POETICS OF READING

P O E T I C S
O F   R E A D I N G

Approaches to the Novel

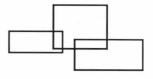

INGE   CROSMAN   WIMMERS

Princeton University Press   Princeton, New Jersey

Copyright © 1988 by Princeton University Press
Published by Princeton University Press
41 William Street, Princeton, New Jersey 08540
In the United Kingdom:
Princeton University Press, Guildford, Surrey
All Rights Reserved
This book has been composed in Palatino
Clothbound editions of Princeton University Press
books are printed on acid-free paper, and binding
materials are chosen for strength and durability
Paperbacks, although satisfactory for personal col-
lections, are not usually suitable for library rebinding
Printed in the United States of America by Princeton
University Press, Princeton, New Jersey
Library of Congress Cataloging-in-Publication Data
Wimmers, Inge Crosman, 1940-
Poetics of reading.
Bibliography: p.
Includes index.
1. Fiction.   2. French fiction—History and
criticism.   I. Title.
PN3331.W56   1988   801'.953   88-17898
ISBN 0-691-06742-2
ISBN 0-691-01447-7 (pbk.)

For Eric and Christopher

CONTENTS

NOTE ON TRANSLATIONS

To enable all readers to follow my argument and illustrations throughout the book, I have provided translations into English of all foreign-language quotations. I indicate in each case whether the translation is mine or is taken from another source. Quotations from the novels I discuss are first given in the original, followed by translations into English. Quotations from the critical works I cite are given directly in English.

ACKNOWLEDGMENTS

Poetics of Reading took shape over several years. The main concepts I discuss and the literary texts I analyse were first tried and tested in undergraduate and graduate courses I taught at Brown. I greatly benefited from student response and from the response to my papers at professional meetings. Particularly inspiring was the 1980 International Colloquium on Poetics, organized by Michael Riffaterre at Columbia University, where I first presented my ideas in a paper entitled "Poétique de la lecture." Equally stimulating was the MLA forum on "Fiction and its Referents," organized by Peter Brooks in 1981, where I read an early version of what was to become the chapter on Proust.

I am especially grateful to Wolfgang Iser for inviting me to spend a research year at the University of Constance, which enabled me to get a firm grounding in German reader-oriented theories. In 1979 and 1983, the Alexander von Humboldt Foundation provided me with generous research fellowships, for which I am most grateful. I also benefited from grants awarded by the Brown University Travel Fund and the Council for International Studies, which enabled me to do research in Paris.

Once the final version of each chapter was completed, the careful, critical readings of my friend and colleague Albert Salvan and my husband, Eric Wimmers, were of invaluable help to me. A note of special thanks goes to my son Christopher, the youngest reader in the family, for his patient consideration while the book took shape and his valuable help with proofreading.

Further thanks go to Deborah Lee for help with the translations, to Yvonne Morin for typing the manuscript, to Carolyn Wenger for copy editing the manuscript, and to Robert Brown of Princeton University Press for his expert advice throughout the review and publication process.

INTRODUCTION

This study began with the question, What is it to read a novel? The question seemed straightforward enough to me at first, though I knew that to define reading I would have to extricate myself from a jungle of conflicting theories. Whatever the theory, however, reading always seemed to involve both a reader and a text. Or so I thought, until I realized that the very concepts of reader and text were seriously being questioned.

In his provocatively titled *Is There a Text in This Class?* Stanley Fish, for one, expresses such rising skepticism: "In 1970 I was asking the question 'Is the reader or the text the source of meaning?' and the entities presupposed by the question *were* the text and the reader whose independence and stability were thus assumed."[1] Fish now denies the independence of text and reader, subjecting them both to the conventional interpretive practices currently in force in a given community.[2] An even more radical view is expressed by Roland Barthes, who describes a text as something undefinable, without set bound-

1. *Is There a Text in This Class?* (Cambridge, Mass.: Harvard University Press, 1980), p. 1.
2. Ibid., p. 16.

aries, "a methodological field": "While the work is held in the hand, the text is held in language: it exists only as discourse."[3]

Though there is truth in these views, they are unnecessarily one-sided. While the interpretive practices in force are important in shaping the reading of a particular text, the structural features and rhetorical strategies of the given text, as well as the reader's approach to it, need to be reckoned with. While one may agree with Barthes that texts, seen from a certain perspective, are boundless, since they belong to the intertextual,[4] a published text has definite boundaries: not only does it exist between the covers of a book, but it also belongs to a particular literary genre. In turn, the reader's awareness of genre conventions raises certain expectations that condition and thus circumscribe his reading.

With this in mind, I decided to give up theorizing about readers and texts in general to see what happens when actual readers (my students, myself) read novels. However problematic the concepts of text and reader are, I decided to use them, since "to discuss an experience of reading," as Jonathan Culler has convincingly shown, "one must adduce a reader and a text."[5] In choosing the texts, I purposely selected a variety of novels—ranging from seventeenth- to twentieth-century works and from the historical to the experimental—to get a better idea of what kind of texts novels are and to see if different novels make for different kinds of reading.

Though it is easy to be specific about the particular literary texts discussed in the following chapters, it is more difficult to pin down the reader in the various narratives or "stories of reading" presented here.[6] A chameleon-like, complex figure,

3. Roland Barthes, "From Work to Text," in Josué V. Harari, ed., *Textual Strategies* (Ithaca: Cornell University Press, 1979), p. 75.
4. Ibid., p. 77.
5. Jonathan Culler, *On Deconstruction: Theory and Criticism after Structuralism* (Ithaca: Cornell University Press, 1982), p. 74.
6. I am borrowing Jonathan Culler's phrase here to emphasize, as he does, that discussions of reading are, in their own right, fictions, "stories of read-

the reader takes on various guises, including different critical and theoretical perspectives as well as different identities—for instance, a male as opposed to a female reader, a seventeenth- as opposed to a twentieth-century reader, or a particular as opposed to a more general reader. This shift in focus, not only from chapter to chapter but also within a single chapter, is intentional: it is to emphasize and illustrate the importance of the concept of "frames of reference," which, as I shall clarify in Chapter One, is central to my discussion of reading. To summarize and anticipate, I introduce the concept of multiple, interlocking frames of reference to account for the complex, interdependent nature of the various frameworks—cultural, textual, personal—within which a given reading takes place.

Theories of reading differ, especially when it comes to deciding whether more weight should be given to the reader or the text and to what extent one depends on the other. Where we place the emphasis depends on our relationship to literature and the kinds of questions we, as readers, want to ask. By introducing the term "poetics" to describe the reading process, I want to stress the close relationship between text and reader, while at the same time broadening the notion of poetics by taking it beyond the study of the internal features of the text to the structures of exchange between text (the published work) and reader. The completed, final "text" thus comes about through reading; it is constituted in and through the act of reading. As Michel Charles has shown, a text acts on the reader and in turn the reader acts on and within the text.[7] According to this view, texts are neither autonomous objects that call forth responses in the reader nor objects solely constructed by the reader.[8]

The dynamic exchange between reader and text does not be-

---

ing." For instance, in *On Deconstruction* he writes: "To speak of the meaning of the work is to tell a story of reading" (p. 35).

7. Michel Charles, *Rhétorique de la lecture* (Paris: Seuil, 1977), p. 63.

8. Ibid., p. 61.

gin merely at the moment of reading but has already been foreseen and incorporated in the text by its author. In discussing how texts anticipate the presence of their audience, Umberto Eco introduces the concept of the "Model Reader," a kind of possible, general reader authors have in mind in creating their work. It is this image of the reader at the moment of writing that enables the author to set up a culturally based system of reference in the text. In turn, this model reader is expected to be able to deal interpretively with the cultural codes inscribed in the work.[9] What authors presuppose, then, is a certain competence based on previous knowledge— knowledge from *outside* the novel. Readers for whom books are written are not blank pages to be filled during a reading, but rather they carry within, like another text, the knowledge of cultural conventions and the memory of other texts.

Besides assuming such conventional knowledge, novelists create their readers' competence *within* the text, through narrative and discursive strategies. How reading is inscribed in the text so that the reader's role is set up ahead of time is the central point in Michel Charles's *Rhétorique de la lecture*.[10] He shows that the extent to which readers are free or constrained has all been mapped out, so that their freedom is, paradoxically, a "restricted freedom."[11]

That the dynamics of reading is already inscribed in the text is also central to the theory of Michael Riffaterre, whose reader moves through textual and intertextual networks along a path that is largely predetermined. Riffaterre describes reading as a two-tiered process: the reader encounters a number of hurdles in a first, sequential reading, but these hurdles are finally over-

9. Umberto Eco, *The Role of the Reader: Explorations in the Semiotics of Texts* (Bloomington: Indiana University Press, 1979), pp. 7–10.
10. Charles, *Rhétorique de la lecture*, p. 9. Cf. Eco's *The Role of the Reader*, p. 8, where he completes the definition of the model reader by allowing for both conventional and text-generated competence.
11. Ibid., pp. 9, 287.

come in a second, retrospective reading once he has found the key that helps him convert stumbling blocks to significant signs in a "structural decoding."[12]

Another view of text-directed reading is Wolfgang Iser's *The Act of Reading*, which describes a reader able to deal constructively with the inscribed "implied reader," defined as a "network of response-inviting structures, which impel the reader to grasp the text."[13] Iser insists that the implied reader—"a textual structure anticipating the presence of the recipient"— must not be confused with the real reader, whose task is twofold: he must heed the construct of the implied reader laid down for him in the text and accomplish a structural act, the act of comprehension.[14]

Given these views, the reading of novels is at once open and controlled—open, because novels are not finished products but anticipate further action on the reader's part; controlled, because as a "work in movement" (to borrow Eco's expression) novels give us freedom within a space circumscribed by conventions and textual strategies; "*The work in movement* is the possibility of numerous different personal interventions, but it is not an amorphous invitation to indiscriminate participation."[15]

Textual and cultural constraints on reading rule out chaos, but this does not mean that there is one right reading. For one thing, complex texts like novels invite more than one mode of reading, allow for more than one critical approach. For another, deciding beforehand what kind of freedom readers may have or what kind of control texts exercise risks theoretical and analytical foreclosure. Instead, it is far more productive to

12. Michael Riffaterre, *Semiotics of Poetry* (Bloomington: Indiana University Press, 1978), p. 81.
13. Wolfgang Iser, *The Act of Reading: A Theory of Aesthetic Response* (Baltimore: Johns Hopkins University Press, 1978), p. 34.
14. Ibid.
15. Eco, *The Role of the Reader*, p. 62.

work out a flexible poetics to show what readings are possible within a given framework of cultural conventions, textual procedures, and theoretical or personal preferences. We are then in a position to account for both open and closed readings. I am not suggesting that anyone, given such a broadly based poetics, could apply it to a novel and come up with a whole range of possible readings. That would be a never-ending task. What I do mean to suggest is that a workable poetics should make us aware of contexts that shape reading.

This is why I have introduced, as a guiding principle, the notion of frames of reference, which is central to the discussion of the various novels studied below. While some of the analyses stress how texts set up systems of reference—this is most obviously the case in *La Princesse de Clèves* and *A la recherche du temps perdu* where reading models inscribed in the text guide characters and reader alike—others show how additional frames of reference are brought into play by the reader's disposition or historical situation. By bringing in the reader's stance, the complexity of the frames of reference increases, as does the difficulty in describing these additional frames. In Chapters One, Five, and Six, I mention various interpretive models that are being developed to deal with the reader's affective response, in particular, those derived from studies on empathy and role playing. Though in my own analyses I primarily pay attention to how textual features and cultural conventions shape the reader's response, I bring in theories of reading based on empathy, identification, and transference to complement my approach—not only to account for the different stages and strategies of reading, but also to stress the importance of the concept of frames of reference in a poetics of reading. My task is not to study in depth one single aspect of reading or to attempt an all-inclusive, comprehensive reading of a particular novel—an impossible task, since one more reading can always be imagined—but to broaden the notion of poetics in order to arrive at a better understanding of what it is to read novels.

With the introduction of the reader and the context of reading into the realm of poetics, meaning and interpretation are, perforce, brought back into the discussion of literary texts. Such a broadened poetics moves beyond the formal features of the text to a discussion of the systems of reference that enter into a particular reading and shape the reader's response. This expanded notion of poetics forced me to reconsider a number of critical concepts. For instance, the concepts of a text's unity or borders became highly problematic once I included not only the printed page but also the reader's construal of it. In turn, this broadened concept of textuality called for a redefinition of mimesis, and for a new framework for the discussion of truth and fiction, or serious as opposed to nonserious discourse.[16] How these concepts may be viewed anew within the context of a poetics of reading applied to the novel will be taken up in the next chapter and developed in subsequent ones.

The poetics developed in these pages is not confined to the theories of reading and approaches to the novel discussed below; other approaches could easily be included, especially since the concept of frames of reference is crucial to most theories of reading. For instance, according to feminist theory, women are to resist culturally learned, male-oriented reading habits and devise a reading in harmony with their identity. Like all critical stances, a "resisting" reading is based on a construct and constitutes a frame of reference. A flexible poetics should be able to account for the added complexity and tension of such conflicting frames of reference in the reading of novels.

Deconstructive theory is another approach that relies on the concept of frames of reference and is compatible with a flexible

16. For a discussion of how deconstruction has a similar impact on the same and related critical concepts, see Jonathan Culler, *On Deconstruction*, pp. 180–205.

poetics of reading. "Framing," Culler writes in discussing different modes of deconstructive reading, "can be regarded as a frame-up, an interpretive imposition that restricts an object by establishing boundaries."[17] This is one reason why deconstructionists have taken delight in cracking or breaking the frame of reference of previous readings—including reading models inscribed in the text itself—while putting in question their own reading of the text under consideration. For instance, there seems to be a note of triumphant negativity when Paul de Man concludes, in *Blindness and Insight*: "Needless to say, this new interpretation will, in turn, be caught in its own form of blindness."[18] In deconstructive readings, the accent is on misreading: "Deconstructive writings will try to put in question anything that might seem a positive conclusion and will try to make their own stopping points distinctively divided, paradoxical, arbitrary, or indeterminate."[19] My own emphasis, in the readings below, is on the constructive convergence of the multiple frames of reference that come into play. With a slight shift in focus and intention I could have shown, however, that the very models of reading inscribed in *La Princesse de Clèves* and in *A la recherche du temps perdu*—which I found so instructive for characters and readers alike—could be shown to be, given another perspective bent on "the careful teasing out of warring forces of significance within the text,"[20] highly problematic.

Thus stories of reading may differ widely, depending on the frame of reference in which the reading was done, and the system of description—which functions like another frame of reference—used to account for the particular reading experi-

17. Ibid., p. 196.
18. Paul de Man, *Blindness and Insight: Essays in the Rhetoric of Contemporary Criticism* (New York: Oxford University Press, 1971), p. 139.
19. Culler, *On Deconstruction*, pp. 259–60.
20. I am quoting here Barbara Johnson's description of the deconstructive approach in *The Critical Difference: Essays in the Contemporary Rhetoric of Reading* (Baltimore: Johns Hopkins University Press, 1980), p. 5.

ence. Though the context in which a novel may be read is potentially boundless, any particular reading of the work is bound or circumscribed by the frames of reference in force at that time. In the readings below, for instance, I set up the context for reading by combining a discussion of the codes and conventions of reading (semiotic approach) with an analysis of discourse strategies (rhetorical approach), while also paying attention to the situation or context of use (pragmatic and phenomenological approaches).

Since the poetics of reading developed here is based on the reciprocal relationship between reader and text, the focus, in the discussions and analyses below, switches abruptly, at times, from the reader's response to the text to a text-centered focus on the structures of the text. This change in direction is not a procedural inconsistency but an unavoidable part of such a poetics. As Jonathan Culler has pointed out, "The shift back and forth in stories of reading between readers' decisive actions and readers' automatic responses is not a mistake that could be corrected but an essential structural feature of the situation."[21] Equally unavoidable are shifts from a linear to a retrospective reading. Though the primary focus is on a chronological, linear reading to account for the reader's experience as he makes his way through a novel for the first time, I anticipate the future significance, from a retrospective point of view, of certain features of the text that gradually acquire such significance through repetition, emphasis, commentary, or other kinds of reinforcement. Such shifts in focus go hand in hand with a shift from a descriptive to an interpretive discourse.

My discussion of the novels included in this study is in part determined by my own view of reading as outlined here, by my understanding of what a novel is (to be taken up in the next chapter), and the context in which these works were first

---

21. Jonathan Culler puts forth this argument in *On Deconstruction* (p. 73) while insisting, as I do, on the importance of working on two fronts at once.

read. The original setting was a course on the novel during which we applied various approaches to narrative fiction to see which ones were most useful in helping us understand what it is to read a novel. I hope that the readings I now offer will be of value to other readers as they match their own experience with novels to the readings offered here.[22]

22. I am using the term "value" in the sense that Barbara Herrnstein Smith uses it when talking about the ethics of interpretation. She suggests that "it is at least in part as the occasion for individual cognitive activity that literary works acquire value for us" (*On the Margins of Discourse: The Relation of Literature to Language* [Chicago: University of Chicago Press, 1978] p. 154).

POETICS OF READING

O N E

Frames of Reference and the Reader

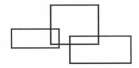

Reading is a complex process that gradually involves us, as we read, in multiple, interlocking "frames of reference." I am borrowing the term from Nelson Goodman who, in *Ways of Worldmaking*, writes: "If I ask about the world, you can offer to tell me how it is under one or more frames of reference; but if I insist that you tell me how it is apart from all frames, what can you say? We are confined to ways of describing whatever is described. Our universe, so to speak, consists of these ways rather than of a world or of worlds."[1] What Goodman says about our experience in the world applies as well to our experience of reading novels and of talking about them. We have no direct, unmediated access to either, since we see both through conventional and conceptual frameworks and talk about them by applying systems of descriptions.

The most fundamental frame of reference in which we begin reading is based on prior knowledge of genre conventions—familiarity, for instance, with what a book is and what kind of book a novel is. This kind of awareness has important consequences, since it presupposes a certain kind of communication

1. Nelson Goodman, *Ways of Worldmaking* (Indianapolis, Ind.: Hackett, 1978), pp. 2–3.

and raises certain kinds of expectation, all of which shape our reading. We know, for instance, that a published book is a corrected, finished text. Though we may respond to it in various ways, its maker cannot, in turn, react to our responses. We also know from literary convention that a book labeled "novel" is a work of fiction. Knowing this prepares us for the kind of communication we are about to enter into and determines our disposition toward the text. For instance, when we open a novel, we know from the start that we are about to enter an imagined world, not one that has any existence prior to or independent of the act of imagination. This knowledge does not, however, protect us from falling prey to the illusion that fictional entities exist or seem real.

In addition to these general, conventional frames of reference, each novel sets up its own frame of reference through narrative discourse and whatever other modes of discourse the narrator may use. Traditionally, it is narrative discourse that constitutes the principal frame of reference at this level. Though the purpose of a narrative is not necessarily to tell a story, readers have learned from tradition to expect a story.[2] Even when a novel frustrates such expectations, the anticipated frame of reference plays a role. It makes us aware of norm breaking and encourages us to piece together a story from even the most disjointed narrative fragments.[3] How ingrained such culturally conditioned attempts at "narrativity"—the reader's story building—are is obvious in novels like

2. That narrators do not merely tell stories but perform verbal acts "in response to—and thus shaped and constrained by—sets of multiple interacting conditions" is discussed by Barbara Herrnstein Smith in "Narrative Versions, Narrative Theories," *Critical Inquiry* 7 (1980): 225–26.

3. Whenever there is an obvious departure from expected norms, there is a marked case of what Mary Louise Pratt has described as "flouting." When confronted with such deviant procedures, the reader knows that there is something to discover; in fact, rule breaking, writes Pratt, can be the point of the utterance (*Toward a Speech Act Theory of Literary Discourse* [Bloomington: Indiana University Press, 1977], pp. 158ff).

Diderot's *Jacques le fataliste* or Robbe-Grillet's *Projet pour une révolution à New York*, both of which frustrate such attempts while also encouraging them.

Built into narrative discourse are several kinds of reference, including references to the story world, to the narrative situation, and to the process or product of narration. Gérard Genette discusses these types of reference in describing the various functions of the narrator in Proust's masterwork. The primary function, according to Genette, is the "narrative function," the telling of the story. Through a second function, the "directing function," the narrator comments on the narrative text and highlights its internal organization. He resorts to a third function, the "function of communication," to command attention, to check the line of communication, thus emphasizing the narrative situation. A fourth function, the "testimonial function," reveals the narrator's attitude (emotional, moral, intellectual) toward his own story, while a fifth, the "ideological function," supplies the reader with authorized commentary on the novel.[4]

Besides these different kinds of reference in a narrator's discourse, the story world itself may be made up of different kinds of entities. For instance, the reader may be referred to entirely imaginary places and characters, ranging from the familiar—in that they are like things and people encountered in the everyday world—to the fantastic and bizarre. Or he may be referred to already existing cultural fictions, including such nonexistent entities as unicorns, fairies, and sorcerers or cultural paradigms of human behavior, such as Don Juan, Faust, or Don Quixote. Of course there are also novels that mix and match historical places, characters, and events with entirely imaginary ones.

4. Gérard Genette, *Narrative Discourse: An Essay in Method*, trans. Jane E. Lewin (Ithaca: Cornell University Press, 1980), pp. 255–57. For the original French version, see Gérard Genette, "Discours du récit," in *Figures III* (Paris: Seuil, 1972), pp. 261–63.

In addition to the self-reflexive reference of discourse and the different kinds of referents that make up story worlds, novels set up intertextual references. The concept of intertextuality is central to several theories of reading, all of which make the point that reference is not from word to world but rather from text to text, and that reading takes place against a backdrop of something already said or written.[5] Reading thus seen as a process of recovering other texts sets up another frame of reference through the constant play of intertextuality.

Michael Riffaterre's theory of reading is built exclusively on intertextuality, defined as "the reader's perception of relationships between a work and others that preceded or followed it. These other texts constitute the intertext of the text in question."[6] According to Riffaterre, the reader cannot help but read intertextually, since the intertext leaves an indelible trace in the text under consideration. He goes so far as to say that intertextuality is at the root of literary experience, that it is the very "mechanism" by which readers read:

> It alone, in effect, produces significance, whereas linear reading, common to both literary and nonliterary texts, produces only meaning. Meaning is merely referential: it results from the relationships, real or imagined, between words and their nonverbal equivalents. Significance, on the other hand, results from the relationships between these same words and verbal systems outside the text (but sometimes partially quoted in the text) and which exist either potentially in language or already actualized in literature.[7]

5. For a discussion of different views on intertextuality, see Jonathan Culler, "Presupposition and Intertextuality," in *The Pursuit of Signs: Semiotics, Literature, Deconstruction* (Ithaca: Cornell University Press, 1981). For current theories of reading in which intertextuality plays a central role, see Riffaterre, *Semiotics of Poetry*, and Gérard Genette, *Palimpsestes* (Paris: Seuil, 1982).

6. Michael Riffaterre, "La Trace de l'intertexte," *La Pensée*, no. 215 (October 1980): 4 (my translation).

7. Michael Riffaterre, "La Syllepse intertextuelle," *Poétique*, no. 40 (1979): 496 (my translation).

Though he admits that readers at first tend to read mimetically (the assumption being that language is referential), he shows that this mimesis is illusory. He concentrates, therefore, on the transformation from referential *meaning* to contextual *significance* through which literary signs that at first were unacceptable referentially acquire significance within a given textual network. He brings in the concept of the "interpretant" to explain how the reader gets from meaning to significance. The kind of mediation through interpretants ranges, he explains, from words that function as dual signs to "hypograms" that function as "texts," since they have an objective existence in the stereotypes of the language or refer the reader to actual texts, either quoted or alluded to.[8] In the final analysis, interpretants are built-in intermediary models between text and intertext that guide and control the reading process since they are all variants of the same structure.[9]

Reading thus viewed is a process of deciphering based on the dialectics of memory between the text under consideration and other texts the reader is being referred to through the mediating models of the interpretant. Intertextuality, then, includes text, intertext, and interpretant in a system of reference strictly based on texts. Though Riffaterre dismisses "ordinary" reference, his theory of reading ultimately brings back the notion of reference, since reading intertextually involves the reader in complex frames of reference.

So far I have mentioned systems of reference ranging from

8. Riffaterre, *Semiotics of Poetry*, pp. 63–64. A "hypogram" may be a single sentence or a string of sentences; it "may be made out of clichés, or it may be a quotation from another text, or a descriptive system" (p. 63). A "descriptive system" is defined as "a network of words associated with one another around a kernel word" (p. 39). The reader can always fill in the gaps, since "each component of the system functions as a metonym of the nucleus" (p. 39).

9. Riffaterre, "Sémiotique intertextuelle: l'interprétant," in *Rhétoriques, sémiotiques*, Collection 10/18 (Paris, 1979), p. 132. It is from Eco's enlarged notion of the interpretant that Riffaterre derives his concept of textual interpretants. See, for example, Eco's *A Theory of Semiotics* (Bloomington: Indiana University Press, 1976), p. 68.

the textual to the intertextual and cultural. Given this view of reading, the reader of novels may be pictured as caught in a web of interlocking frames of reference, some based on cultural conventions, others on textual strategies. To what extent these systems of reference interact with, support, or thwart each other depends largely on the kind of text in question, but also on the kind of reading a text is given, since the particular point of view to which novels are subjected when readers read constitutes yet another frame of reference. For instance, some theories of reading literature take readers beyond textual borders by encouraging them to extend interpretation to include self-interpretation. Over ten years ago, Paul Ricoeur spoke of "appropriating" the text while introducing such a concept of interpretation: "By appropriation, I mean this, that the interpretation of a text is completed in the self-interpretation of a subject who henceforth understands himself better, who understands himself differently, or who even begins to understand himself."[10] Reading reflexively, in Ricoeur's view, opens up texts, "actualizes" them, constitutes them as an event in time, and gives them their ultimate meaning (*signification*): "Reading is concretized in an act which is to the text what speech is to language, that is, an event and the very process of discourse. The text only had meaning, that is to say internal relationships, a structure; it now has significance, that is to say, it produces an effect within the reading subject's very discourse."[11] It is through such self-reflexive acts of reading, as Ricoeur shows, that texts acquire a context while the suspended reference toward the world and an audience is once more set in motion.[12]

10. Paul Ricoeur, "Qu'est-ce qu'un texte?" in *Hermeneutik und Dialektik, Festschrift* in honor of H. G. Gadamer, ed. Rüdiger Bubner et al. (Tübingen: Mohr, 1970), 2:194–95, my translation here and below. See also Ricoeur's more recent *Temps et récit* (Paris: Seuil, 1983), 1:85–109, for more detail on the intersection of the world of the text and the world of the reader.
11. Ibid., p. 196.
12. Ibid., p. 195.

More recently, Wolfgang Iser has similarly described reading as an event, an experience. In developing his theory of aesthetic response, he takes a close look at what kind of experience reading actually is, and how it is linked to other realms of our experience: "Through gestalt-forming, we actually participate in the text, and.this means that we are caught up in the very thing we are producing. This is why we often have the impression, as we read, that we are living another life."[13] In turn, this experience of being in the text has important repercussions on our life experience: "Through the experience of the text . . . something happens to our own store of experience" (p. 132). Iser specifies that this new experience is not simply an adding on to what we already know, but, rather, that "it is a restructuring of what we already possess" (p. 132). He dramatizes what happens to the reader by sketching a dialogic exchange between text and reader and between the reader's former and present self: "Our assimilation of the alien experience must have retroactive effects on that store of experience" (p. 155). He concludes that reading is a process of "becoming conscious," and he extends the framework of interpretation from text to reader, stressing that there is more than one kind of significance that comes into play: "The constitution of meaning not only implies the creation of a totality emerging from interacting textual perspectives . . . but also, through formulating this totality, it enables us to formulate ourselves and thus discover an inner world of which we had hitherto not been conscious" (p. 158).

While reading, as Iser has shown, plays a role in shaping our lives, conversely, the kind of experiences we bring to texts influences our reading. How and to what extent the reader's own experience enters into the reading process is the central question in Anselm Haverkamp's theory of reading. He fo-

13. Iser, *The Act of Reading*, p. 127. Further references in this chapter are given parenthetically in the text.

cuses on the structure of exchange (*Transferstruktur*) between text and reader in a "participatory" reading. While the text, through its aesthetic structures, invites the reader to play a certain role, it is the reader's disposition that actually determines what shape this role will take. According to Haverkamp, the reader's disposition depends primarily on the reader's recognition of analogies between the fictional world and his own life experience. Such a process of identification gives the reader the illusion of a participatory reading. Haverkamp concludes by calling for a "rhetoric of empathy," since he sees empathy as the primary hermeneutic function, necessary to bring about the illusions set up through fiction.[14]

To view reading as self-exploration is not merely a frame of reference applied to literature by theorists. Writers themselves have inscribed such reading models in their work. One of the most explicit and persuasive invitations to transworld reading is found in Proust's *A la recherche du temps perdu*:

> En réalité, chaque lecteur est, quand il lit, le propre lecteur de soi–même. L'ouvrage de l'écrivain n'est qu'une espèce d'instrument optique qu'il offre au lecteur afin de lui permettre de discerner ce que, sans ce livre, il n'eût peut-être pas vu en soi-même. La reconnaissance en soi-même, par le lecteur, de ce que dit le livre, est la preuve de la vérité de celui-ci, et *vice versa*, au moins dans une certaine mesure, la différence entre les deux textes pouvant être souvent imputée non à l'auteur mais au lecteur.[15]

> In reality every reader is, while he is reading, the reader of his own self. The writer's work is merely a kind of op-

14. Anselm Haverkamp, "Illusion und Empathie: Die Struktur der 'teilnehmenden Lektüre' in den *Leiden Werthers*, in *Erzählforschung*, ed. Eberhard Lämmert (Stuttgart: Metzler, 1981), pp. 243–68.

15. Proust, *A la recherche du temps perdu*, Bibliothèque de la Pléiade (Paris: Gallimard, 1954), 3:911. The English translation that follows is from *Remembrance of Things Past*, trans. C. K. Scott Moncrieff, Terence Kilmartin, and Andreas Mayor (New York: Random House, 1981), 3:949.

tical instrument which he offers to the reader to enable him to discern what, without this book, he would perhaps never have perceived in himself. And the recognition by the reader in his own self of what the book says is the proof of its veracity, the contrary also being true, at least to a certain extent, for the difference between the two texts may sometimes be imputed less to the author than to the reader.

The Proustian narrator extends literary reference beyond the written word by inviting the reader to test the work's "veracity" against the background of a second "text," the reader's life experience. In doing so, he teaches us that the borders between fictional and actual worlds are not absolute.

Proust, like the theorists who extend text interpretation to self-exploration, encourages us to consider what kinds of fiction novels are and the impact they have on us. He thus raises a central question that plays a role in our reading of novels even when our attention is not directly focused on the nature of fiction. We may view novels as world making, for instance, as does Nelson Goodman: "Works of fiction in literature and their counterparts in other arts obviously play a prominent role in worldmaking; our worlds are no more a heritage from scientists, biographers, and historians than from novelists, playwrights, and painters."[16] Though art may be viewed as world making, we should keep in mind that it is a special kind of world that is thus created, distinct from the "actual" world in that it has no existence outside of our imagination.

Yet fictional worlds are not entirely cut off from the actual world. Experience in one is carried over, in part at least, to the other. What does come into play, for instance, as we read novels, is our dependence on discourse conventions and conceptual categories. Joseph Margolis, for example, points out that, whether authors or readers, "we can never, in practice or prin-

16. Goodman, *Ways of Worldmaking*, p. 103.

ciple, free the features of a fictional world from *some* conceptual dependence (however limited and indeterminate it may
be) on the conditions of coherence, the causal order, and the
normal features of the phenomena of what we regard as the
actual world."[17] Similarly, how we interpret discourse in the
novel depends to a certain extent on the ways we speak in and
about the real world. Whether we take what a narrator or character says as playful or serious, as straightforward or ironic, as
narrative or some other kind of discourse, depends largely on
our familiarity with the conventions of speaking or writing. In
this respect, there is no absolute line of demarcation between
a fictional world and the "real" world.

It is clear that novels, though different and separate from
the "actual" world, intersect with it in more than one way by
drawing on the reader's previous knowledge. Another point
worth making is that all we find in novels is not necessarily to
be taken as make-believe or, in Searle's words, "pretended
speech acts." Searle himself came close to admitting this when
he spoke of the need to study "how the author conveys a serious speech act through the performance of the pretended
speech acts which constitute the work of fiction."[18] What is
problematic is Searle's assumption that there is a categorical
difference between discourse in the novel and elsewhere, the
"real" world. He argues, for instance, that "the pretended il-
locutions which constitute a work of fiction are made possible
by the existence of a set of conventions which suspend the
normal operations of the rules relating illocutionary acts to the
world."[19]

In response to Searle's argument, Stanley Fish insists that
this shared pretense exists not only in fiction but in discourse

17. Joseph Margolis, "The Logic and Structures of Fictional Discourse," *Philosophy and Literature* 7 (1983): 162–81.
18. John R. Searle, "The Logical Status of Fictional Discourse," *New Literary
History* 6 (1975): 332.
19. Ibid. p. 326.

in general: "Shared pretense is what enables us to talk about anything at all"; in fact, "such pretenses proliferate and make the world."[20] While Fish agrees with Searle that it is right to distinguish between serious and fictional discourse on the basis of "internal canons of criticism," he does not go along with Searle's claim that serious discourse entails a responsibility to facts as they really are. Instead he claims that "the rules and conventions under which speakers and hearers 'normally' operate don't demand that language be faithful to the facts; rather, they specify the shape of that fidelity . . . creating it, rather than enforcing it."[21] Fish concludes that the crucial distinction between serious and fictional discourse is not "between the real and the not-so-real; rather it is one between two systems of discourse conventions which certainly can be differentiated, but not on a scale of reality."[22]

Though we may well agree with Fish that saying makes it so, a crucial distinction remains, and that is the overall context in which we read novels, knowing that a novel, by definition, is a work of fiction. This outermost frame of reference sets up from the start a certain kind of communication with the reader, based on genre rules and conventions of reading. Another distinction worth making is between *what* is told and *how* it is told. For instance, I cannot agree with Barbara Herrnstein Smith when, in speaking of novels, she writes: "It is the *act* of reporting events, the *act* of describing persons and referring to places that is fictive. The novel *represents* the verbal action of a man reporting, describing, and referring."[23] What is "fictive" in the sense of "make-believe" is the gradual elaboration of the fictional world with its made-up setting, characters, and events. What is actually taking place is the act of narration and

20. Stanley Fish, "How to Do Things with Austin and Searle: Speech Act Theory and Literary Criticism," *MLN* 91 (1976): 1022.
21. Ibid., 1018.
22. Ibid., 1019.
23. Smith, *On the Margins of Discourse*, p. 29.

referring. Narrators do not *pretend* to narrate, they actually *do* narrate, and they refer to the world they have created without pretending.

It should also be kept in mind that the discourse of novels is not confined to setting up and talking about the fictional world: narrative discourse can give way to explanatory, didactic, ideological, or other modes of discourse. A striking example is Proust's novel, in which the narrator continually interrupts his story to philosophize. When he does so, he does not give the impression that he is pretending. He speaks in earnest, following the conventions of serious discourse, and the reader is bound to take it as such. It is against the background of such modes of speech in the novel that one must evaluate Searle's claim that serious speech acts may be found in works of fiction and that not necessarily all references in a work of fiction are "pretended acts of referring," that some are "real references."[24]

Acknowledging the presence of earnest or "serious" discourse in novels raises the problematic question of the status of truth in fiction. How truth is defined will, of course, determine any discussion of it. If it is viewed in the narrow, absolute sense in which truth must correspond to existence (a view familiar from Aristotle to Augustine and, more recently, to Käthe Hamburger), then there is not much that can be done with this concept in the realm of fiction.[25] Hamburger, for instance, defines truth as "that which is the case,"[26] as nonrelative, nonsubjective, and absolute,[27] and she concludes that the notion of truth cannot be applied to aesthetic works, because they are subject to plural interpretations,[28] and because verifi-

24. Searle, "Logical Status of Fictional Discourse," p. 332.
25. Käthe Hamburger, *Wahrheit und ästhetische Wahrheit* (Stuttgart: Klett and Cotta, 1979).
26. Ibid., p. 128.
27. Ibid., p. 131.
28. Ibid., p. 137.

cation procedures cannot be applied to them. Quite another view is put forth by Hans Georg Gadamer, who believes in the "philosophical significance" of art, since, according to him, we can find truth through a work of art that we could not find in any other way.[29] When introducing the concept of truth into the reading of novels, we should keep in mind what Vaihinger has said about judgments in general: "A fictive judgment cannot give us a theoretical, absolute truth, but only a practical, relative one, a truth that is only 'right' in relation to the speaker and the purpose he has in mind."[30]

Whatever our concept of truth, we may well wonder if it is one of the frames of reference we are likely to invoke when reading novels. One answer would be to point out, as Foucault has done, that since the will to truth is so powerful in shaping and controlling Western discourse, we have been conditioned to read and interpret within this framework: "I believe that this will to truth—leaning in this way on a support and an institutional distribution—tends to exert a sort of pressure and something like power of constraint (I am still speaking of our own society) on other discourses. I am thinking of the way in which for centuries Western literature sought to ground itself on the natural, the 'vraisemblable', on sincerity, on science as well—in short, on 'true' discourse."[31] If we believe that society and culture have set us up to expect, desire, and look for truth, then we cannot ignore this dimension of reading and writing.[32] Nor can we ignore it if the quest for

29. Hans Georg Gadamer, *Wahrheit und Methode* (Tübingen: Mohr, 1965), p. xiv.

30. Hans Vaihinger, *Die Philosophie des Als Ob* (Leipzig: Felix Meiner, 1920), p. 603, my translation. Since truth is relative, Nelson Goodman suggests that the concept of truth should be subsumed under the general notion of "rightness of fit" (*Ways of Worldmaking*, p. 132).

31. Michel Foucault, "The Order of Discourse," in Robert Young, ed., *Untying the Text* (Boston: Routledge and Kegan Paul, 1981), p. 55.

32. Finding truth in a novel may well be what gives it value for many a reader. That we cannot ignore the fact that we evaluate aesthetic works, much as we

truth has been built into the text we are reading; or if the text is designed in such a way that readers are given the impression that what is said or portrayed is true.

That the impression of truth is an important force in Western literary theory and practice is obvious from the attention it has been given in discussions on writing and reading. Known under many guises, it has been called verisimilitude (*vraisemblance*), referential illusion (*l'illusion de mimésis* or *l'illusion référentielle*), and reality effect (*l'effect de réel* or *l'illusion réaliste*). Genette, among others, has warned that the impression of direct reference while reading narrative fiction is indeed an illusion (the illusion being that the words on the page refer to the world), since narration is the province of language, and since language signifies without imitating:

> No narrative can "show" or "imitate" the story it tells. All it can do is tell it in a manner which is detailed, precise, "alive," and in that way give more or less the *illusion of mimesis*—which is the only narrative mimesis, for this single and sufficient reason: that narration, oral or written, is a fact of language, and language signifies without imitating.[33]

Like Genette, Barthes too argues that it is all a matter of language, that the referential illusion is built up through words. What he calls the "reality effect" (*l'effet de réel*) is created, as he

---

evaluate other things in life, has been convincingly shown by Barbara Herrnstein Smith in "Contingencies of Value," *Critical Inquiry* 10 (1983): 1–35. She claims that "to exist is to evaluate" (p. 19), and that literary and aesthetic value, like other kinds of value, are mutable and diverse. Since value, like truth, is relative—depending on cultural contexts and a subject's needs, interests, and resources—it must be viewed within flexible, adjustable frames of reference. This has not been done, as Smith shows, by critical theory, since it has been in quest of transcendence, endurance, and universality. As a result, it "has been unable to acknowledge the most fundamental character of literary value, which is mutability and diversity" (p. 10).

33. Genette, *Narrative Discourse*, p. 164. For the original French text, see *Figures III*, p. 185.

sees it, by seemingly irrelevant or insignificant details whose main raison d'être is to create the illusion of "that's how it was." This referential illusion comes about, as Barthes points out, through the direct collusion of the referent and the signifier in a process of signification that brackets the signified:

> The truth of this illusion is the following: excluded from realist expression by virtue of being a signified of denotation, the "real" returns as a signified of connotation; because the very moment these details seem to directly denote the real, they do nothing else, without saying so, but to signify it: Flaubert's barometer, Michelet's little door finally say nothing other than: *we are the real.*[34]

Presentation, then, must not be confused with representation: "The reality of the text is not the text of reality."[35] Barthes, in speaking of the "erosion of the signified,"[36] claims, as Genette does, that words cannot imitate the real, but, rather, the representational system of the real.[37]

An *effet de réel* subjecting the reader to a powerful referential illusion can be created, as I will show in the following chapters, in more ways than one, ranging from the impact of details to persuasive narrative strategies and the compelling coherence of a tightly woven fictional universe. I shall, therefore, use the term *effet de réel* in a broader sense, taking it beyond Barthes's rather narrow application in order to include other "reality effects." In this broader sense, *effet de réel* stands op-

34. Roland Barthes, "L'Effet de réel," *Communications* 11 (1968): 88 (my translation). A word of caution regarding the function of descriptive details is in order. Mieke Bal has pointed out, for instance, that description is an integral part of a novel's action or plot, and that Barthes has shortchanged the function of details by claiming that all they do is to say "we are the real." See her *Narratologie* (Paris: Klinksieck, 1977), pp. 90–109.
35. My translation of Claude Duchet's statement, "Le réel du texte n'est pas le texte du réel," in *Le Réel et le texte* (Paris: Armand Colin, 1974), p. 7.
36. Barthes, "L'Effet de réel," p. 88.
37. Gérard Genette, "Frontières du récit," in *Figures II* (Paris: Seuil, 1969), pp. 53–55.

posed to *effet de fiction*, which draws attention to the fictionality of the text, thus destroying, rather than reinforcing, the referential illusion.[38]

Barthes himself, in another context where he discusses historical discourse, considers other ways of creating the impression of verisimilitude. For instance, he describes how concealing the narrating voice is one way of achieving such an effect: "At the level of discourse, objectivity, or the absence of any clues to the narrator, turns out to be a particular form of fiction, the result of what might be called the referential illusion, where the historian tries to give the impression that the referent is speaking for itself. This illusion is not confined to historical discourse: novelists galore, in the days of realism, considered themselves 'objective,' because they had suppressed all traces of the *I* in their text."[39]

Benveniste has analyzed the traces that point to the very operation of narrating. They are forms like "I," "you," "here," "there," "now," and the use of the present tense. Contrariwise, the act of narration is veiled through the use of "he," "she," "they," and the past tense, so that the reader is under the spell of the illusion that nobody speaks, that reality itself speaks.[40]

The reality effect can also be achieved through redundancy and circularity, as Jacques Neef has shown in the case of Flaubert. For instance, he points out that the relationship between characters and their setting is tautological, since descriptive details have been chosen precisely for one purpose: to reveal the characters' psychological makeup. Moreover, he shows how the majority of Flaubert's comparisons and metaphors

38. Others have used the term *effet de réel* in this broader sense. See, for example, Gérard Cordesse, "Note sur l'énonciation narrative," *Poétique* 65 (1986): 45.
39. Roland Barthes, "Historical Discourse," in *Introduction to Structuralism*, ed. Michael Lane (New York: Basic Books, 1970), p. 149.
40. Emile Benveniste, *Problèmes de linguistique générale* (Paris: Gallimard, 1966), pp. 251–57.

grow out of the story universe, thus giving the reader familiar with this universe the impression that they are just and pertinent. Cultural and ideological references are also convincing, because they refer the reader not to historical reality but to all that is "intelligible in a given era, the read and the readable of a culture."[41] They seem true, since they are rooted in a culture's familiar conventions. For Neef, the reality illusion is not merely or primarily based on the representational power of language, as Genette and Barthes have argued, but on what he callls "the figural workings of language" through which the realist text turns representation into figuration.[42] This is made possible, as he shows, through a process of internal motivation and highlighting whereby the text dissimulates the arbitrary nature of narration while giving unquestionable authority to the story.[43]

Though we may pinpoint the various narrative strategies responsible for creating referential illusions, we cannot simply dismiss such illusions because we know about them. As Gombrich has shrewdly pointed out, "though we may be intellectually aware of the fact that any given experience *must* be an illusion, we cannot, strictly speaking, watch ourselves having an illusion."[44] What we know in theory to be an illusion is quite another thing while we are immersed in the experience of reading. Why this is so depends not only on the illusion building of textual strategies but also on our attitude toward narrative fiction. Kendall L. Walton, for instance, holds the view that we bring a special disposition to the reading of novels: "We feel a psychological bond to fictions, an intimacy with them, of a kind which otherwise we feel only toward what we

41. Jacques Neef, "La Figuration réaliste," *Poétique*, no. 16 (1973), p. 472, my translation.
42. Ibid., p. 475.
43. Ibid., pp. 474–75.
44. E. H. Gombrich, *Art and Illusion*, Bollingen Series (Princeton: Princeton University Press, 1972), p. 5.

take to be actual. Fictions, unlike objects of other intensional attitudes, are in this way thought of as though they exist. We have a strong tendency to regard them as part of our reality, despite our knowledge that they are not."[45] Walton points out that this is not simply "suspension of disbelief," since readers of fiction have a dual standpoint, existing at once literally (actually) and fictionally, viewing the fictional world both from inside and outside: "We don't promote fictions to the level of reality, but we descend to the level of fiction where we 'share' worlds with fictional characters."[46] This leaves the reader of novels in the same paradoxical situation Ricoeur has described for the reader of metaphors: there is tension, since the reader oscillates between two frames of reference, between *is* (figuratively) and *is not* (literally).[47]

All this suggests that there is no insurmountable barrier between the fictional and the actual, since both are intimately linked to our experience as a whole. The dichotomy between art and life, as René Wellek showed some years ago, just does not hold up:

> Art is "illusion," "fiction," the world changed into language, paint or sound. It seems to me an oddity of our time that this simple insight into the aesthetic fact is construed as a denial of the relevance, the humanity and sig-

45. Kendall L. Walton, "How Remote Are Fictional Worlds from the Real World?" *Journal of Aesthetics and Art Criticism* 37 (1978–1979): 19. For quite a different view on the matter, see Johannes Anderegg, who makes a categorical distinction between the reading of pragmatic texts (*Sachtext*) and fictional texts (*Fiktivtext*), claiming that a pragmatic text refers to a state of affairs that exists independently of the text whereas fictional texts create their own "fictive frames of reference" (*Bezugsfeld*). According to Anderegg, it is during the act of reading that the reader gradually "overcomes his own frame of reference through the constitution of the fictional reference" (*Fiktion und Kommunikation: Ein Beitrag zur Theorie der Prosa*, 2d ed. [Göttingen: Vandenhoeck and Ruprecht, 1977], p. 107, my translation).

46. Walton, "How Remote Are Fictional Worlds?" p. 21.

47. Paul Ricoeur, *La Métaphore vive* (Paris: Seuil, 1975), p. 321.

nificance of art. The recognition of the difference between life and art, of the "ontological gap" between a product of the mind, a linguistic structure, and the events in "real" life which it reflects, does not and cannot mean that the work of art is a mere empty play of forms, cut off from reality. The relation of art to reality is not as simple as older naturalistic theories of copying or "imitation" or Marxist "mirroring" assume. "Realism" is not the only method of art. It excludes three-quarters of the world's literature. It minimizes the role of imagination, personality "making."[48]

Novels, then, are not simply verbal constructs whose illusion building we can rationally dismiss; they are experienced as events while they engage us in a particular process of world building, feeling, and thinking. As such, they acquire meaning while interpretation takes us beyond the borders of the text. Though the fictional world of novels is not an actual world—it does not exist in the ordinary sense—it can take on dimensions of the real, ranging from the illusory *effet de réel* to impressions of the real brought about through the reader's active participation in filling in gaps or in identifying, through empathy, with fictional experience.

Given the complexity of reading, it seems that a workable poetics should be comprehensive enough to account for the multiple dimensions of reading, paying attention to the various frames of reference that come into play and that, through their intersection, make up the literary referent. Since the reading of novels involves the reader in complex systems of reference and inference, the literary referent gradually emerges during the reading process through textual guidance and the reader's active collaboration. Seen this way, the literary referent is an "interpretant" and not reference to a prior

48. René Wellek, "Some Principles of Criticism," in *The Critical Moment* (London: Faber and Faber, 1963), pp. 41–42.

state of affairs, and it includes both the conceptual and affective dimensions of reading. It is only through a retrospective, global reading of a text that a reader can locate the various systems of reference that make up the literary referent, since in a first, sequential reading he is caught in and participates in a shifting network of multiple, intersecting frames of reference.

The various frames of reference I have outlined in this chapter all play a significant role in the reading of narrative fiction. In presenting these systems of reference, I have purposely included different theoretical positions to set up as flexible a poetics as possible. Most of these approaches are complementary, either because they deal with different stages or aspects of reading, or because they bring into focus, though from different perspectives, the same or related concepts. Depending on the novel, certain frames of reference are more dominant than others, yet the dynamics of reading is always built up through their intersection. For instance, cultural conventions and taboos constitute a powerful frame of reference in the reading of both *La Princesse de Clèves* and *Projet pour une révolution à New York*; yet, to understand the tension that gradually builds up, we must resort to a second frame of reference, narrative discourse, to see how it revises or undermines these conventions. Similarly, while narrative strategy supplies the relevant frame of reference for reading *Madame Bovary*, its full impact can only be felt if we read intertextually, evaluating the narrative against the background of literary and cultural stereotypes. Moreover, for the reader to be able to perceive and evaluate innovations in narrative technique presupposes previous knowledge of the norm and the ability to read from a certain critical distance. My readings in the following chapters presuppose such a reader. They also assume that the reader's personal frame of reference plays an important part in a poetics of reading.

To take a closer look at the interplay of frames of reference, and to test what has been said about referential illusion as a "fact" of reading, I will begin with a close reading of *La Princesse de Clèves*, a seventeenth-century novel in which fictional, historical, and cultural references are closely linked through narrative discourse, all at the service of verisimilitude. While going on in subsequent chapters to study other, quite different novels, it will be revealing to see how identifying the various systems of reference in a given novel allows us to distinguish between different kinds of novels and the readings they make possible.

T W O

Rewriting *vraisemblance* in *La Princesse de Clèves*

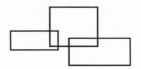

Bienséance, non pas ce qui est honnête, mais ce qui convient aux personnes.—CHAPELAIN, *De la poésie représentative*

When *La Princesse de Clèves* was first published in March 1678, it gave rise to lively discussions. Of major interest in these first responses to the book was the behavior of its central character, the princess. A telling example is the poll organized by *Le Mercure Galant* that asked its readers whether Mme. de Clèves was right to tell her husband about her love for the duc de Nemours. The majority thought not. Her conduct seemed implausible, since according to social custom (the well-established code of *bienséance*), such behavior was not sanctioned.[1] Readers of the time did not ask themselves whether the princess's conduct was possible, but, rather, whether it was likely. Only what seemed plausible when judged within the context

---

1. René Bray shows how the notions of *vraisemblance* and *bienséance* both rely on conformity to public opinion and respect of the norm, and that both have moral and aesthetic connotations. In speaking of *vraisemblance* he writes: "On joint sous le même vocable des conseils moraux, des préceptes techniques, et des principes esthétiques" ("In the same vocable are joined moral counsels, technical precepts and aesthetic principles") (*Formation de la doctrine classique* [Paris: Nizet, 1927], p. 206, my translation).

of contemporary social custom was likely to be taken as *vraisemblance*. The official view in this regard is summed up in a revealing statement made by Nicole in *De la vraie beauté*: "Il ne faut ni regarder les choses comme elles sont en elles-mêmes, ni telles que les sait celui qui parle ou qui écrit, mais par rapport seulement à ce qu'en savent ceux qui lisent ou qui entendent"[2] ("One must not look at things as they are in themselves, nor as they are known to the speaker or the writer, but only with regard to that which is known by readers or listeners").

The question of verisimilitude was taken up once more in a book published at the end of that same year written by a certain Valincour: *Lettres à Madame la Marquise de*** sur le sujet de la Princesse de Clèves*.[3] In a telling passage the author of these letters recounts a conversation he had concerning the pros and cons of the *Princesse de Clèves*. His opponent points out that the book falls short because it does not respect the basic rules of fiction, which stipulate that a work of literature should either be all invented or situated within a consistent historical framework. By introducing purely imaginary characters (Mme. and Mlle. de Chartres) into a historical setting (the court of Henri II), and by falsifying historical data (the duc de Clèves, for instance, was never married and was not of marriageable age in 1558), the book shocks its readers, so argues the opponent, by transgressing conventional expectations.[4]

The lesson we learn from this "critical" debate on *La Princesse de Clèves* is that it is important to bear in mind the context in which a book is read or judged. What is obvious from the

---

2. Quoted in *Formation de la doctrine classique*, p. 208, my translation.

3. References here are to a later edition of the *Lettres* by A. Cazes (Paris: Editions Bossard, 1926). The continued interest in the subject is obvious from another publication that was soon to follow in 1679, L'abbé de Charnes's *Conversations sur la critique de la Princesse de Clèves*. A more recent, excellent volume of critical responses to the novel is Maurice Laugaa's *Lectures de Mme de Lafayette* (Paris: Armand Colin, 1971).

4. Valincour, *Lettres*, pp. 132–148.

Valincour collection and the poll published in *Le Mercure Gal-lant* is that most negative pronouncements on the characters were primarily based on contemporary literary canons and the accepted code of behavior. It is amazing how few readers paid attention to the actual text of the novel.[5] Had they read closely, they would have noticed that one of the central interpretative problems they kept solving over and over, namely, whether or not Mme. de Clèves's confession was plausible, had already been solved, since her extraordinary conduct is repeatedly emphasized and "naturalized" within the text itself. The princess herself is the first to call attention to her unusual behavior by prefacing her confession with these mediating remarks, which prepare both her husband and the reader for what is to come: "Je vais vous faire un aveu que l'on n'a jamais fait à son mari; mais l'innocence de ma conduite et de mes intentions m'en donne la force"[6] ("I am going to make you a confession such as no woman has ever made to her husband; the innocence of my actions and of my intentions gives me strength to do so"). What could be more explicit than this built-in interpretive glossing, which overtly tells us that Mme. de Clèves is well aware of what is done and what is not—a fictional fact worth noting for the evaluation of her character and conduct.

Not only is the message explicit, it is also emphatic, through style and repetition. Twice, while evaluating her course of action in the presence of her husband, Mme. de Clèves uses the

5. Valincour was one of the first to point out that some things happened in the novel for reasons of narrative economy. Gérard Genette continues this line of argument in his article "Vraisemblance et motivation," *Communications* 11 (1968): 5–21.

6. *La Princesse de Clèves* (Cambridge, Mass.: Integral Editions, 1969), p. 96. This is an excellent edition, with helpful notes on the historical and cultural context in which the book was written and read. The English translation that follows is from the anonymous translation, *The Princess of Clèves*, published in *Seven French Short Novel Masterpieces* (New York: Popular Library, 1965), p. 89. Hereafter, unless otherwise specified, page references to both these sources are given sequentially within parentheses, for example (p. 96; translation, p. 89).

word *jamais* to underscore the unique nature of her frank admission. The first time she speaks of "un aveu que l'on n'a jamais fait à son mari" ("a confession such as no woman has ever made to her husband") (p. 96; my translation). The second time, she says, "Il n'y a pas dans le monde une autre aventure pareille à la mienne; il n'y a point une autre femme capable de la même chose. Le hasard ne peut l'avoir fait inventer; on ne l'a *jamais* imaginée et cette pensée n'est *jamais* tombée dans un autre esprit que le mien" ("In the whole world there is not another case like mine; there is not another woman capable of doing what I have done! Chance could not make any one invent it; no one has ever imagined it,—the very thought never entered any one's mind but mine") (p. 110, my italics; translation, p. 101). Besides such emphatic statements, the repeated characterization of the confession as "extraordinary" highlights its unusual nature. No fewer than five other times Mme. de Clèves describes her confession as "la singularité d'un pareil aveu"("the strangeness of such a confession") (p. 99; translation, p. 91), "une chose si extraordinaire" ("such an extraordinary thing") (p. 109; translation, p. 100), "la confiance extraordinaire ou, pour mieux dire, folle que j'ai eue en vous" ("the extraordinary, I might say foolish, confidence I had in you") (p. 110; translation, p. 101), and "un procédé aussi extraordinaire que le mien" ("such extraordinary conduct as mine") (p. 125; translation, p. 112). Nor should we forget that the first time she thinks of undertaking such a confession, she rejects it as "crazy": "ensuite elle fut étonnée de l'avoir eue, elle y trouva de la folie, et retomba dans l'embarras de ne savoir quel parti prendre" ("then she was astonished that the thought occurred to her: she deemed it madness, and fell back into the agony of indecision") (p. 67; translation, p. 65). Through such remarks, the narrator stresses from the start the princess's paradoxical situation, subject to both a rigorous social code and the exacting demands of her own personality.

In addition to the thoughts and remarks from Mme. de Clèves's own point of view, one of the most revealing clues comes from the duc de Nemours; as secret witness of the confessional scene, he not only gives a reading of Mme. de Clèves's conduct, "un remède si extraordinaire" ("this desperate remedy") (p. 98; translation, p. 90), but foreshadows what is to come by anticipating the princess's final resolution to withdraw, many pages before it is actually made: "Il fit réflexion . . . qu'il était impossible d'engager une personne qui avait recours à un remède si extraordinaire" ("He reflected that it was impossible to gain any influence over a woman who resorted to so strange a remedy") (pp. 99–100; translation, p. 92). This reflection by a character functions as an effective reading model and is part of the rhetorical strategies that set up a tightly knit, persuasive narrative.

Yet it is clear that such interpretive comments and reading models were not heeded by most seventeenth-century readers. More important, in their minds, were the powerful conventions of *bienséance* and *vraisemblance*. This insistent cultural frame of reference entered into direct conflict with the text's emphatic rhetorical strategies. Although the narrator explicitly presents the princess's behavior as extraordinary—hence implausible under ordinary circumstances—and uses rhetorical mediation to take the reader gently from conventional to unconventional conduct, the *aveu* was not accepted. The modern reader, on the other hand, may wonder why such a fuss was made over it. What surprises us today is not the princess's behavior, but the many justifications for it. What we learn from them, however, is the importance of the codes of *bienséance* and *vraisemblance* so crucial to an understanding of the frame of mind and behavior of the novel's central character. Our awareness of these codes in turn provides us with the logical background necessary for understanding the elaborate rhetorical framework set up by the narrator. The built-in justifications also allow us to infer the kind of reader inscribed in *La*

Princesse de Clèves,[7] and enable us to see the extent of the difference, in belief and attitude, between the projected seventeenth-century reader and his twentieth-century counterpart. One obvious difference is that today's readers are more likely to be swayed by the narrator's rhetorical manipulation in reference to the *aveu*: by openly flouting conventions and justifying unconventional conduct, he strengthens the impression of verisimilitude; he appears to be saying that the true order is not to be found in social convention but in the story he is telling.[8] Such an *effet de réel* was not likely to work for the seventeenth-century reader subject to the tyranny of *bienséance*.

Because of such marked differences in reading and responding to this novel, I make a distinction, whenever necessary, between the seventeenth- and twentieth-century reader. What these differences emphasize is the importance of the concept of frames of reference in a poetics of reading. They also illustrate how the dynamics of reading is built up through the intersection of several systems of reference, where some dominate while others are subordinate. It is interesting to see, by comparing present-day readings with those from another century, how the frames of reference and the order of their importance change over time. While I mention some of these changes in this chapter, my main focus is on a more general, transhistorical reader in order to show how Mme. de La Fayette takes pains to make the unconventional believable by closely joining the various frames of reference that shape the reading of the novel—the rhetorical, cultural, and historical—

7. Gerald Prince discusses various manifestations of the narratee in his excellent ground-breaking article, "Introduction à l'étude du narrataire," *Poétique* 14 (1973): 178–96. See also Gérard Genette, *Nouveau discours du récit* (Paris: Seuil, 1983), pp. 90–93.

8. How the text reinforces its own authority by exposing its departures from the norm is discussed by Jonathan Culler in *Structuralist Poetics* (Ithaca: Cornell University Press, 1975), pp. 148ff. He calls this type of verisimilitude "the conventionally natural" and discusses it in relation to four other kinds of *vraisemblance* (pp. 140–60).

all calculated to create and reinforce the same illusion: the *effet de réel*.

As previously noted, narrative logic is built up through evaluation, explanation, and justification of the heroine's unconventional conduct. To set up a persuasive rhetorical framework, the narrator uses yet another strategy: he refers the reader to his own experience in a number of passages that imply shared knowledge about love. The repeated use of the demonstrative *ce* is an obvious sign that the reader is being referred to a common frame of reference. Whether such a framework exists, or whether the implicit reference is filled in by the reader, is another matter. What counts is that such a mode of communication is set up in the novel, and that it invites reader participation. For instance, what is implied in the following passage, in which the narrator describes M. de Nemours's behavior, is that the reader knows about passionate love: "M. de Nemours sentait pour elle une inclination violente qui lui donnait *cette* douceur et *cet* enjouement qu'inspirent les premiers désirs de plaire"[9] (M. de Nemours felt for her a strong inclination which gave him *that* sweetness and playfulness called forth by the first desire to please) (p. 26; my translation). In a later passage, Nemours, still timid in Mme. de Clèves's presence, "s'assit vis-à-vis d'elle, avec *cette* crainte et *cette* timidité que donnent les véritables passions" ("sat down opposite her, with *that* uneasiness and timidity that comes from real passion") (p. 56; my translation). General knowledge about love is again implied in such elliptical descriptions to be filled in by the reader as "*ce* charme qui ne se trouve que dans l'amour" ("all the sweetness that only love can give") (p. 132; translation, pp. 91–92) and "*cette* joie que donne la présence de ce que l'on aime" ("*that* joy which the presence of one's beloved inspires") (pp. 91–92; my translation).

9. My italics, here and in the next few sentences.

Through this kind of complicity, the narrator sets up structures of response between text and reader that reinforce the
effet de réel.[10] Though readers may well be aware of the fictional
status of novels, they look nonetheless for a certain corre-
spondence between reality and the fictions they are immersed
in, especially when encouraged to do so by the text in hand. I
therefore cannot agree with Gérard Genette's claim that it is
senseless to wonder about the motive behind Mme. de
Clèves's confession because, according to him, her feelings
"are not real feelings but feelings of fiction and of language,"
and that as such they are "confined to all the utterances
through which discourse signifies them."[11] In making such
claims, Genette gives the reading of narrative fiction too narrow a scope. The point is that *through* Mme. de Clèves—despite the fact that she is a character in a universe made up of
words—the reader is given insight into a complex human situation, and that he participates in setting up a framework for
viewing, understanding, and judging such human behavior
here and elsewhere.

Besides heightening the *effet de réel* by drawing readers into
a participatory reading through references that imply shared
knowledge, narrator and characters alike repeatedly refer to
history and to contemporary society. Such references were
particularly effective in the seventeenth century, given the
conventions of reading and writing in force at the time. *La
Princesse de Clèves* appeared in the literary climate of the *nouvelle galante* and the *nouvelle historique*, at a time when concern
for verisimilitude through exact detail was in vogue.[12] Novel-

10. Such responses may include a process of identification based on empathy
as described by Anselm Haverkamp in "Illusion und Empathie." According to
Haverkamp, this kind of participatory reading is based on the reader's recognition of analogies between his life experience and the experiences described
in the story world.

11. My translation from Genette, "Vraisemblance et motivation," p. 14 n. 1.

12. Important publications that precede *La Princesse de Clèves* include Segrais's
Nouvelles françaises (1658) and Mme. de Villedieu's *Journal amoureux* and her

ists turned to history and society in search of subject matter, so that a considerable part of each novel presented contemporary readers with familiar cultural references. Though history is carefully linked to the main intrigue in *La Princesse de Clèves*, one can understand why some readers criticized Mme. de La Fayette for inaccuracies of historical detail. They were factually correct but strayed from the central purpose of the book by insisting on history as the major frame of reference. The seventeenth-century reader was likely to do so, because of his great interest in historical detail and his habit of judging novels like histories. At the time, the two genres did not much differ in focus and style. Both novelists and historians featured the passions of great men, reinforcing the current belief that passions were at the very root of historical change. The distinction between history and fiction was further blurred by the historians' practice of guessing at or inventing the psychological motivations of their heroes and freely substituting fiction for historical fact.[13]

Since a faithful history of the times was not her main objective, Mme. de La Fayette had no scruples about inventing two fictional characters (Mme. and Mlle. de Chartres), or about changing the age of a historical personage (M. de Clèves was a child in 1558) and the character of another (the duc de Nemours was not a steadfast lover as portrayed in the novel but an incorrigible Don Juan). The author made these changes to suit her own purpose of building up the central intrigue. Though ancillary to this aim, the historical framework of the novel plays an important role in the reading experience. Our first contact with the historical dimension of the book is almost overwhelming, since in the short space of about ten pages we

---

Annales galantes (1670), all characterized by exactness of detail in a historical setting.

13. For a discussion of the fictional dimension of such historical accounts, see Barbara Woshinsky, *La Princesse de Clèves: The Tension of Elegance* (The Hague: Mouton, 1973), p. 48.

are presented with a historical milieu (the court of Henri II) while we are given brief portraits, one by one, of the principal dignitaries of Europe, including a quick look at their intricate network of genealogical and political alliances, interspersed with some of their private and public feats.[14]

Though these historical names do not set up direct references to past reality, since they are embedded in a fictional world where different norms of reception obtain,[15] they do have well-known cultural connotations for the informed reader. How and to what extent these come into play during the act of reading depends in part on the reader and in part on the particular text he is reading. A reader may be more or less familiar with a given historical or geographical reference, and what comes to mind may be influenced by the text's focus on particular aspects of the "reality" referred to.[16] Whatever the case, it is important to realize that well-known names function differently in a reading than ordinary names or words, since they bring with them certain cultural connotations. We are

14. Mme. de La Fayette did careful research on the life of the Valois court. Her major source of information was Brantôme, according to a detailed study of her historical sources by Henri Chamard and Gustave Rudler, "Les Sources historiques de *La Princesse de Clèves*," *Revue du XVIème Siècle* 2 (1914): 93–105.

15. That it is not different ways of referring that distinguishes fictional texts from pragmatic ones but, rather, different norms of reception, is discussed by Rainer Wimmer in *Referenzsemantik* (Tübingen: Max Niemeyer Verlag, 1979), p. 175.

16. Umberto Eco, for instance, shows how the name "Napoleon" "denotes a cultural unit which is well defined and which finds a place in a semantic field of historical entities" (*A Theory of Semiotics*, p. 87). He points out that different cultures may attribute different *connotations* to historical names, while their *denotations* remain the same—unlike proper names of unknown persons, which have open denotations (p. 88). Françoise van Rossum-Guyon, on the other hand, makes the point that it is through language that readers imagine extratextual reality referred to in a novel. For instance, she shows how, in Balzac's description of Angoulême, geographical, historical, sociological, and psychological signifieds all acquire meaning through the relationship the author establishes between them and the work as a whole, so that it is the author and not reality that determines what shape the town will take for the reader (*Critique du roman* [Paris: Gallimard, 1970], p. 55).

more easily prey to referential illusion when the work we are reading abounds in historical or geographical detail, evoking a whole era or milieu.

While the modern reader of *La Princesse de Clèves* has to strain his memory to place the historical figures, the seventeenth-century reader must have had quite a different experience, since the people and events referred to were part of his recent past and quite familiar to him. In fact, for the aristocratic reader of the time, the novel's setting must have been "a ceremony of recognition."[17] The invention of intimate secrets concerning his forebears, and the alteration of geneological or historical fact, must have seemed at once irreverent and enticing (the reader as voyeur while secret intimacies are offered for public inspection).

Referential illusion has a strong impact on the reader of *La Princesse de Clèves*, not only because he is presented with a long list of historical figures and a detailed account of sixteenth-century court intrigues at the time of Henri II, but also because he is given a close look at manners, etiquette, and customs. It is important to note that Mme. de La Fayette combined two historical periods by endowing the court of Henri II with the manners and customs of the court of Louis XIV. While the modern reader is hardly aware of the chronological discrepancy, seventeenth-century readers must have been. Yet they did not object to this transgression. It is likely that they felt more at home with and convinced by the familiar code of behavior, a frame of reference so important at the time. The *effet de réel* created by the historical setting and reinforced by detailed accounts of customs and intrigues at court, is subsequently maintained through the constant interaction between fictional and historical characters in the same familiar setting, and the repeated interpolation of historical facts and events into the fictional universe. By making a world out of both his-

17. Woshinsky, *La Princesse de Clèves: The Tension of Elegance*, p. 58.

torical and fictional building blocks, Mme. de La Fayette creates some special effects: historical figures seem more familiar and alive in the behind-the-scenes conversations and activities of the fictional world; conversely, fictional characters begin to seem more "real" as they are repeatedly seen in the presence of historical figures, participating in well-known ceremonies and events. In fact, it would be difficult for the reader to make a conscious distinction between historical and fictional characters, since they are intricately linked through narrative discourse.

It is remarkable how the illusion of reality is reinforced through careful manipulation of story and discourse. The narrator adopts a matter-of-fact way of telling and describing that is used throughout the novel and equally applied to both history and invention. Besides unity of style, he observes unity of manner; private affairs are depicted with the same care as historical events. In describing both, the narrator pays attention to relevant detail, gives convincing documentation or explanations, and observes logical connections by providing consistency and coherence, all of which reinforces the impression of verisimilitude while making it impossible for the reader to determine from the novel itself where history stops and fiction begins.

The reality effect is heightened in the scenes in which the narrator sets up a situation of complicity with the reader by inviting him to bring in a piece of shared historical knowledge. One example of such complicity between narrator and reader, who obviously know more than the sixteenth-century characters portrayed (what is future from their perspective has already come to pass), involves a tête-à-tête between Mme. de Clèves and Mary Stuart—a historical character whose fate was well known to every educated seventeenth-century reader. In concluding her account of the unhappy life of her mother (Marie de Lorraine), Mary Stuart adds these foreboding remarks: "On dit que je lui ressemble; je crains de lui ressembler aussi par sa malheureuse destinée" ("I am told that I am like her; I dread the same sad fate") (p. 19; translation, p. 28). Since the reader knows that what she fears will turn out to be true, he reads Mlle. de Chartres's reassuring response from the distance of dramatic irony, sharing with the narrator the elevated position of those who know:[18] "Mlle de Chartres dit à la reine que ces tristes pressentiments étaient si mal fondés qu'elle ne les conserverait pas longtemps, et qu'elle ne devait point douter que son bonheur ne répondit aux apparences" ("Mademoiselle de Chartres assured the crown princess that these gloomy presentiments were so fantastic that they could not long surprise her, and that she ought not to doubt that her good fortune would give the lie to her fears") (p. 19; translation, p. 28). Even the reader who is not familiar enough with history to know that Mary Stuart was executed by Elizabeth I will view Mlle. de Chartres's naive assurance with wry amusement, since she does not heed her recent lesson, the story just told her by Mary Stuart, which is a piece of actual history, full of political intrigue and treachery.[19]

The close ties between history and fiction are particularly evident in passages where a sentimental episode grows out of a historical one while both are intricately joined within the same narrative framework. For example, in one instance the narrator begins by giving a detailed account—closely based on a historical source—of a discussion in the king's presence about the validity of horoscopes and fortunetelling.[20] While the king concludes that these predictions cannot amount to much, M.

18. Wayne Booth discusses the reader's position in the reading of ironic texts in *A Rhetoric of Irony* (Chicago: University of Chicago Press, 1975), pp. 33–44.
19. The story about Marie de Lorraine is taken from a historical source. According to Henri Chamard and Gustave Rudler, Mme. de La Fayette telescoped two passages from Pierre Matthieu's *Histoire de France* ("Les Sources historiques," pp. 114–16).
20. The historical source is Jean Le Laboureur's edition of the *Mémoires* of Michel de Castelnau. See Chamard and Rudler, "Les Sources historiques," pp. 96–97.

de Nemours replies that he too has little ground to believe in astrology, because—and now he whispers the rest to Mme. de Clèves, who alone is within earshot—"On m'a prédit . . . que je serais heureux par les bontés de la personne du monde pour qui j'aurais la plus violente et la plus respectueuse passion. Vous pouvez juger, madame, si je dois croire aux prédictions" ("I was told that I should be made happy by the kindness of the woman for whom I should have the most violent and the most respectful passion. You may judge, Madame, whether I ought to believe in predictions") (p. 60; translation, p. 60). Nemours's contribution to the discussion on astrology is entirely fictional, yet any reader who has not done research on the available historical documents could not possibly tell the dividing line between fact and fiction, for both are closely linked under the same topic (fortunetelling), in the same situational context (a conversation at court), and through the same narrative rendering (direct quotation of character speech). Mme. de La Fayette thus adjusts the documentary source to suit her own purpose and exploits it fully to further the novel's central intrigue, the growing love between the duc de Nemours and Mme. de Clèves. The reader's attention is entirely focused on the personal when the omniscient narrator intrudes into Mme. de Clèves's mind to show how quick she is to decipher the duke's veiled declaration of love.[21] The reader thus fully participates in the dramatic impact of the growing tension and suspense by being a witness to the characters' conversation and thoughts.

By thus closely joining history and invention in a convincing narrative to further her fictional intrigue, Mme. de La Fayette creates a strong *effet de réel*. This impression is further strength-

21. Dorrit Cohn uses the term "psycho-narration" to designate one of the techniques for rendering consciousness in third-person narratives. She defines psycho-narration as the narrator's omniscient description of a character's consciousness (*Transparent Minds: Narrative Modes for Presenting Consciousness in Fiction* [Princeton: Princeton University Press, 1978], pp. 11–12).

ened when she adapts her material to the interests and tastes of her public, thereby following the dictates of *bienséance* and *vraisemblance*. For instance, she leaves out two major historical events of sixteenth-century France—the Renaissance and the Reformation—and focuses instead on gallantry, etiquette, and ceremony, all so important to the court of Louis XIV.[22]

Her editing of historical sources is always in keeping with classical taste and style: she cuts judiciously by eliminating crude or useless details, adds explanations where necessary, and reverses the sequence of events for logical or artistic reasons, thus building up a coherent, well-structured text. In keeping with classical style, she substitutes succinct, generalizing descriptions for detailed, particularizing ones. For example, Brantôme lists all the various exercises in which the duc de Nemours excels, while Mme. de La Fayette simply talks about "une adresse extraordinaire dans tous ses exercices" ("he was unusually skilful in physical exercises") (p. 5; translation, p. 17). In fact, she usually deletes or attenuates the colorful, individual traits she found in the historical portrayals of her characters.[23] The reader has to imagine what is meant when Mary Stuart is described as "parfaite pour l'esprit et pour le corps" ("faultless in mind and body") (p. 2; translation, p. 16), Elisabeth de France, as "cette incomparable beauté" ("that unrivalled beauty") (p. 2; translation, p. 26), and M. de Nemours, as "un chef-d'oeuvre de la nature" ("a masterpiece of Nature") (p. 5; translation, p. 17). Descriptions of the court are equally abstract and hyperbolic. While the modern reader may well wonder what is meant when he learns that the court of Henri II stands out because of its *magni-*

22. Chamard and Rudler suggest that Mme. de La Fayette may have ignored the Reformation for political reasons, while her silence about the Renaissance may be explained by seventeenth-century prejudice ("La Couleur historique dans *La Princesse de Clèves*," *Revue du XVIème Siècle* 5 [1917]: 1–5).

23. For a comparative study of the descriptive style of the historical sources in Mme. de La Fayette's novel, see ibid., pp. 16–19.

ficence, *galanterie*, and *grandeur*, the seventeenth-century reader was not likely to question this description; he would simply fill in the blanks with conventional connotations. Nor was the contemporary reader likely to object to the scarcity of concrete detail, since he was used to idealized description, both in novels and in historical writings.

The extensive use of historical and cultural references has an important function in creating the impression of verisimilitude so important to the author's central purpose, producing a convincing account of an unusual person in an unusual situation. Equally important is the intensifying focus on the inner life of Mme. de Clèves, which initiates the reader into her way of thinking and feeling. Though we know that other people's thoughts and feelings are inaccessible to us, and that novelists who depict them are fabricating, it is nonetheless true, as Dorrit Cohn has shown, that the "special life-likeness of narrative fiction . . . depends on what writers and readers know least in life: how another mind thinks, another body feels."[24] To understand how the reader is gradually initiated into Mme. de Clèves's dilemma and how it is made believable, we must take a closer look at the principal joints of the novel's rhetorical framework. When we do so, we realize that through foregrounding, repetition, and built-in interpretive models, the author sets up the interpretive framework for reading the novel.

Besides the title, which calls attention to the central character, Mlle. de Chartres—soon to become the Princesse de Clèves—stands out in the gallery of portraits that opens the novel. It is significant that the only other person singled out is the duc de Nemours, so that the reader may jump to the conclusion that these two exceptional people are made for each other. In fact, the narrator draws this conclusion for the reader

24. Cohn, *Transparent Minds*, pp. 5–6. The author also discusses how the mimesis of consciousness contributed to the growing trend of narrative realism.

while describing their first meeting at the ball: "De sorte que, se voyant souvent, et se voyant l'un et l'autre ce qu'il y avait de plus parfait à la cour, il était difficile qu'ils ne se plussent infiniment" ("Since they met often, and found each other more attractive than any one else at court, they naturally experienced great delight in being together") (p. 26; translation, p. 33).

That the private life of the princess is at the center of the book becomes more and more obvious as the reading progresses. The focus is on Mlle. de Chartres once the historical cadre has been set up, and we soon see that the entire narrative is built around her: all episodes and events are linked to her, while the narrative focus is increasingly centered on her inner life through summary narration of her consciousness, through narrated and quoted monologues, and through dialogue in which she reveals her thoughts directly. We are also given inside information into anything that plays a role in her moral and sentimental education. For example, we are first-hand witnesses of the moral guidance given her by her mother and husband; we hear each of the four stories told to her about problematic aspects of love; we are given verbatim the entire text of the lost letter through which she learns all about betrayal and jealousy; and we follow each step of her relationship with the duc de Nemours. At crucial moments, we are given insights into her reactions and inner debate, so that we are in a position to understand her unusual confession to her husband and her final, unshakable decision to withdraw from the life of passions—a decision arrived at through close reasoning witnessed by the reader, who becomes familiar with all the evidence on which such an irrevocable decision is based.

What is striking in the initial presentation of Mlle. de Chartres is that most of the long paragraph devoted to her gives a rather detailed account of her upbringing, in particular, her mother's teaching about love. The full impact of these lessons on both reader and character is obvious at a second reading. They explain her moral dilemma when she falls in love, and help the reader to understand her future conduct. At this early stage of the reading they constitute an interpretive model, since every detail mentioned acquires significance later on. This passage contains, in essence, the moral and senti-mental education of Mme. de Clèves, since experience will reinforce her mother's teachings. It thus foreshadows what is to come, while repetition drives home the message:[25]

> Elle faisait souvent à sa fille des peintures de l'amour; elle lui montrait ce qu'il a d'agréable pour la persuader plus aisément sur ce qu'elle lui en apprenait de dangereux; elle lui contait le peu de sincérité des hommes, leurs tromperies et leur infidélité, les malheurs domestiques où plongent les engagements; et elle lui faisait voir, d'un autre côté, quelle tranquillité suivait la vie d'une honnête femme, et combien la vertu donnait d'éclat et d'élévation à une personne qui avait de la beauté et de la naissance; mais elle lui faisait voir aussi combien il était difficile de conserver cette vertu, que par une extrême défiance de soi-même et par un grand soin de s'attacher à ce qui seul peut faire le bonheur d'une femme, qui est d'aimer son mari et d'en être aimée.

> She often drew pictures of love to her daughter, showing her its fascinations, in order to give her a better under-standing of its perils. She told her how insincere men are, how false and deceitful; she described the domestic mis-eries which illicit love-affairs entail, and, on the other hand, pictured to her the peaceful happiness of a virtuous

---

25. In her reading of this novel from a feminist perspective, Marianne Hirsch underlines the importance of the mother-daughter relationship: "A Mother's Discourse: Incorporation and Repetition in *La Princesse de Clèves*," *Yale French Studies*, no. 62 (1981): 68. Similarly, Nancy K. Miller has stressed the impor-tance of maternal discourse in the novel's internal motivation. See her "Em-phasis Added: Plots and Plausibilities in Women's Fiction," *PMLA* 96 (1981): 39.

woman's life, as well as the distinction and elevation which virtue gives to a woman of rank and beauty. She taught her, too, how hard it was to preserve this virtue without extreme care, and without that one sure means of securing a wife's happiness, which is to love her husband and to be loved by him. (p. 10; translation, p. 21)

The negative aspects of love that Mme. de Chartres singles out in her teaching—insincerity, infidelity, loss of tranquility—will turn out to be of major concern to Mme. de Clèves once she has fallen in love, especially since everything she hears confirms this negative view. For example, Mme. de Chartres, pursuing her role as moral guide, tells her a story about intrigues of love and deception at court and, noticing her daughter's inclination for M. de Nemours, is quick to paint a negative image of the duke: "Elle lui en dit du bien et y mêla beaucoup de louanges empoisonnées sur la sagesse qu'il avait d'être incapable de devenir amoureux et sur ce qu'il ne se faisait qu'un plaisir et non pas un attachement sérieux du commerce des femmes" ("She spoke of him in warm terms, but craftily praised his discretion in being unable to fall really in love and in seeking only pleasure, not a serious attachment, in his relations with women") (p. 37; translation, p. 42). This Don Juan image of Nemours, reinforced one page later by the dauphine, "il avait un nombre infini de maîtresses" ("he had an infinite number of mistresses") (p. 38; translation, p. 43), begins to undermine her faith in love and strikes the first spark of jealousy, which sets in motion her inner turmoil.

It is revealing that her first troubling encounter with love leads her at once to the decision to tell Mme. de Chartres about it.[26] Although this first decision to "confess" is not carried out because of her mother's sudden illness, it is symptomatic of the future pattern of her behavior. The reader has

26. *La Princesse de Clèves*, p. 38.

time to get used to the idea before the first uncustomary confession actually occurs.

Her mother's parting lesson, which presents the dangers of love in dramatic terms, increases her inner turmoil. It also gives her renewed moral strength by reminding her of her duty to her husband and to herself. This lesson stands out in the text, since it takes up nearly a page on which the mother's words are quoted verbatim so that character and reader alike get the full benefit. This emphasis is functional, as was the first lesson, since the mother's advice for the future conduct of her daughter prefigures the daughter's actions: "Ayez de la force et du courage, ma fille, retirez-vous de la cour, obligez votre mari de vous emmener; ne craignez point de prendre des partis trop rudes et trop difficiles, quelque affreux qu'ils vous paraissent d'abord: ils seront plus doux dans les suites que les malheurs d'une galanterie" ("Take strength and courage, my daughter: withdraw from the court; compel your husband to take you away. Do not be afraid of making a difficult decision. Terrible as it may appear at first, it will in the end be pleasanter than the consequences of a love-affair") (p. 41; translation, p. 45). Her flight from society and her confession to her husband—both difficult and crude solutions not sanctioned by the prevailing social code—are thus encouraged and prepared for by Mme. de Chartres's final words. Once again, the groundwork is laid for a course of action, which is logically and strategically prepared for through this built-in reading of a difficult situation.

It comes as no surprise that after the death of her mother, Mme. de Clèves, feeling utterly abandoned and in dire need of guidance in the midst of a moral dilemma, turns to her husband for help. He takes over where Mme. de Chartres left off. While he loses ground as husband, he gains influence as adviser and confidant. His role is now strikingly similar to the mother's. This parallelism is emphasized through narrative pattern: like Mme. de Chartres, he tells a story about an unhappy love affair; he encourages Mme. de Clèves to turn to him for help and advice; and he gives her his views on love just before he dies.

The unhappy story M. de Clèves tells his wife is the novel's second major story within the story. Once again, the principal narrator lets the characters speak directly, so that the reader witnesses the story at their level, without outside mediation. While M. de Clèves is the story's chief narrator and Mme. de Clèves the listener, he at times interpolates the speech of his characters through direct and indirect discourse. The narrator's effacement in both the principal and secondary stories gives the reader direct contact with a variety of views and feelings not filtered through the narrator's consciousness or language.

M. de Clèves's story is closely linked to the foregoing narrative account: the people he talks about are from the same time and place (the court of Henri II) as those of the principal narrative. Though his story is about the private life of two people—the love affair between M. de Clèves's friend Sancerre and Mme. de Tournon—it has an exemplary function, since it gives the reader and Mme. de Clèves another close look at how people in love behave. Mme. de Tournon's deceptive conduct—pretending to mourn her husband while having an affair with Sancerre, and in turn pretending to love Sancerre while secretly making marriage plans with another—confirms Mme. de Chartres's lesson about masked appearances at court where *être* and *paraître* cannot easily be distinguished.

Mme. de Clèves is deeply troubled by this account of the dishonesty of someone she respects highly. Her reaction is interpolated into the story, thus calling attention once more to the novel's principal character and confirming the reader's impression that events are organized with her in mind. The most obvious shift from secondary story to central character occurs in a passage in which the principal narrator omnisciently intrudes to interpolate Mme. de Clèves's reaction into M. de Clèves's story at a crucial point. A reader who has al-

ready read the novel once is aware of the functional significance of this passage for the novel's further development: M.
de Clèves's "ode to sincerity," told to Sancerre and here repeated verbatim for his listener, makes a memorable impression on her and eventually guides her toward the controversial
confession:[27]

> Je vous donne, lui dis-je, le conseil que je prendrais
> pour moi-même; car la sincérité me touche d'une telle
> sorte que je crois que si ma maîtresse, et même ma
> femme, m'avouait que quelqu'un lui plût, j'en serais af-
> fligé sans en être aigri. Je quitterais le personnage d'amant
> ou de mari, pour la conseiller et pour la plaindre.
>
> Ces paroles firent rougir Madame de Clèves, et elle y
> trouva un certain rapport avec l'état où elle était, qui la
> surprit et qui lui donna un trouble dont elle fut longtemps
> à se remettre.

> I give you the advice, I said to him, which I should take
> myself; for I am so touched by sincerity that I believe that
> if my mistress, or my wife, were to confess that any one
> pleased her, I should be distressed without being an-
> gered, and should lay aside the character of lover or hus-
> band to advise and sympathize with her.
>
> At these words Madame de Clèves blushed, finding a
> certain likeness to her own condition which surprised her
> and distressed her for some time. (p. 47; translation, p. 49)

The importance of M. de Clèves's advice to Sancerre is apparent at a first reading, not only because he repeats word for
word to his wife what he has told Sancerre, but also because

27. That she remembers her husband's plea for sincerity is explicitly stated
later on: "Ce que M. de Clèves lui avait dit sur la sincérité, en parlant de
Madame de Tournon, lui revint dans l'esprit; il lui sembla qu'elle lui devait
avouer l'inclination qu'elle avait pour M. de Nemours" ("She remembered
what her husband had said about her sincerity when he was speaking about
Madame de Tournon, and it seemed to her that it was her duty to confess her
passion for Monsieur de Nemours") (p. 67; translation, p. 65).

his plea for sincerity is conspicuously set off in a paragraph of its own. In the same way, attention is given to Mme. de Clèves's reaction, which also constitutes a separate paragraph. Such *mise en relief* prefigures the importance of this passage for the development both of events in the storyworld and the reader's interpretive constructs.

Besides the advice and moral guidance received from mother and husband, two additional stories within the story play a significant role in the princess's sentimental education. As in the previous stories, the emphasis is on love's inconstancy and the pain caused by jealousy. None of these secondary stories is superfluous, since each of them serves the same function: to focus attention on the problems of love, and, in turn, on the impact of new insights on Mme. de Clèves. The reader is bound to be sensitive to such narrative overdetermination through repetition of the same pattern.

The third story is told by the dauphine to Mme. de Clèves and other ladies at court, to familiarize them with the life and background of Queen Elizabeth I. Though the story is historical, filled with facts about Henry VIII and Ann Boleyn, the focus is, once more, on private matters—the inconstancy of love and the terrors of jealously, which are even more boundless in this story filled with murderous revenge.[28]

The fourth story, about infidelity and untrustworthiness, is told by the vidame de Chartres to the duc de Nemours in order to retrieve the controversial love letter that everyone, including Mme. de Clèves, attributes to M. de Nemours. To clear himself, the duke tells the story to Mme. de Clèves, whose reaction becomes the focus of the narrative: her inner turmoil, caused by jealousy, immediately gives way to a state

28. This story, like the story about Mme. de Valentinois, is based on historical research. According to Chamard and Rudler, Mme. de La Fayette got most of her information from Sanderus and Le Laboureur (Chamard and Rudler, "Les Sources historiques," pp. 307 ff.). Once again, the historical intertext is woven into the fictional plot.

of newly recovered calm and joy once the duke is beyond suspicion.

The repeated focus on the same character makes it obvious that incidents, like that of the lost letter, and interpolated stories all acquire meaning in relation to her. Even narrative technique is closely geared to the progressive stages of her self-awareness. Whereas in the beginning of the book the predominant mode is omniscient narration of her inner life, there is a marked difference after the episode of the lost letter. The reader is suddenly given insight into her mind through a more direct method, either through quoted interior monologue, which is the most direct way of rendering consciousness, or through narrated monologue, the *style indirect libre*, allowing the character's mental speech to infiltrate the narrator's discourse.[29]

The most revealing passage is the one describing Mme. de Clèves's state of consciousness just after she has realized that the change in her attitude toward M. de Nemours is a sign of her passion for him. It is remarkable how, in one and the same paragraph, the narrator's omniscient narration of her consciousness suddenly switches to an interior monologue just as the princess, at a moment of rare insight, fully comprehends her situation and is able to put it in a broader perspective and settle on a plan of action that foreshadows her future attitude and conduct. The successive moments of insight and the accompanying changes in mode of narration make the passage worth quoting in its entirety:

> Elle avait ignoré jusqu'alors les inquiétudes mortelles de la défiance et de la jalousie; elle n'avait pensé qu'à se défendre d'aimer M. de Nemours et elle n'avait point encore commencé à craindre qu'il en aimât une autre. Quoique les soupçons que lui avait donnés cette lettre fussent ef-

29. For a discussion of these modes of narration, see Cohn, *Transparent Minds*, pp. 11–17.

facés, ils ne laissèrent pas de lui ouvrir les yeux sur le hasard d'être trompée et de lui donner des impressions de
défiance et de jalousie qu'elle n'avait jamais eues. Elle fut
étonnée de n'avoir point encore pensé combien il était peu
vraisemblable qu'un homme comme M. de Nemours, qui
avait toujours fait paraître tant de légèreté parmi les
femmes, fût capable d'un attachement sincère et durable.
Elle trouva qu'il était presque impossible qu'elle pût être
contente de sa passion. Mais quand je le pourrais être, di-
sait-elle, qu'en veux-je faire? Veux-je la souffrir? Veux-je y
répondre? Veux-je m'engager dans une galanterie? Veux-
je manquer à M. de Clèves? Veux-je me manquer à moi-
même? Et veux-je enfin m'exposer aux cruels repentirs et
aux mortelles douleurs que donne l'amour? Je suis vain-
cue et surmontée par une inclination qui m'entraîne
malgré moi. Toutes mes résolutions sont inutiles; je pen-
sai hier tout ce que je pense aujourd'hui et je fais aujour-
d'hui tout le contraire de ce que je résolus hier. Il faut
m'arracher de la présence de M. de Nemours; il faut m'en
aller à la campagne, quelque bizarre que puisse paraître
mon voyage; et si M. de Clèves s'opiniâtre à l'empêcher
ou à en vouloir savoir les raisons, peut-être lui ferai-je
mal, et à moi-même aussi, de les lui apprendre.

Up to that time she had not known the stings of mistrust and jealousy; her only thought had been to keep
from loving Monsieur de Nemours, and she had not yet
begun to fear that he loved another. Although the suspi-
cions that this letter had aroused were wholly removed,
they opened her eyes to the danger of being deceived,
and gave her impressions of mistrust and jealousy such as
she had never felt before. She was astounded that she had
never yet thought how improbable it was that a man like
Monsieur de Nemours, who had always treated women
with such fickleness, should be capable of a sincere and

lasting attachment. She thought it almost impossible that she could ever be satisfied with his love. "But if I could be," she asked herself, "what could I do with it? Do I wish it? Could I return it? Do I wish to begin a love-affair? Do I wish to fail in my duty to Monsieur de Clèves? Do I wish to expose myself to the cruel repentance and mortal anguish that are inseparable from love? I am overwhelmed by an affection which carries me away in spite of myself; all my resolutions are vain; I thought yesterday what I think to-day, and I act to-day in direct contradition to my resolutions of yesterday. I must tear myself away from the society of Monsieur de Nemours; I must go to the country, strange as the trip may seem; and if Monsieur de Clèves persists in opposing it, or in demanding my reasons, perhaps I shall do him and myself the wrong of telling them to him. (pp. 92–93; translation, p. 86)

From this detailed account of her inner life it is obvious that this moment of self-awareness is of capital importance. It also provides the key for all further developments in the novel by initiating the pattern of flight and entrapment, which dominates the episodic structure of the rest of the book. One of the first consequences of her flight from love is the confession to her husband, which, in turn, sets up a vicious causal chain leading to his death. This unexpected event prompts M. de Nemours to pursue her further by asking for her hand, a final temptation that she escapes by withdrawing to a far-off country estate and, finally, by entering a convent.

It is significant that the word the narrator most frequently uses to describe her frame of mind after her first step toward self-awareness is *trouble*. This emphasis on her inner turmoil lays the groundwork for one of her major arguments for retreat from love, inner calm (*repos*). Ironically, by pursuing her, the duc de Nemours continually revives this troubling state, which plays such an important role in her final choice. By giving us insight into her emotional state and by familiarizing us with her reasoning, the narrator deeply implicates us in her situation: we not only learn to trust her judgment but also build up a fair amount of sympathy for her inner struggle. When she renounces love, we are likely to understand and empathize, not condemn her.

Suffering through jealousy is obviously her main reason for retreat and is rhetorically (vis-à-vis Nemours, vis-à-vis the reader) her strongest point, since she backs up her reasoning with concrete detail. By bringing in inconstancy, she draws on her experience, all she has seen and heard, which as readers we have witnessed along with her. Yet throughout her "debate" with the duke, she repeatedly brings in a second reason, duty to her husband. She closely links the two reasons to reinforce her argument. That she does this not only to convince her interlocutor but to strengthen her own decision is quite apparent in her final attempt to persuade. Here she quite frankly admits, in reply to M. de Nemours's objection that he cannot see how her "austere virtue" can oppose her feelings any longer, that she finds herself in a paradoxical situation in which she is constantly torn between scruples and the desire to love. Through direct quotation of her speech, the reader is allowed to follow each step of her reasoning and to fully share the emotional impact. Her choice of words and syntax, and the chiasmic development of her argument, constitute a persuasive verbal translation of the no-exit situation in which she finds herself:

> —Je sais bien qu'il n'y a rien de plus difficile que ce que j'entreprends, répliqua Mme de Clèves; je me défie de mes forces au milieu de mes raisons. Ce que je crois devoir à la mémoire de M. de Clèves serait faible s'il n'était soutenu par l'intérêt de mon repos; et les raisons de mon repos ont besoin d'être soutenues de celles de mon devoir. Mais, quoique je me défie de moi-même, je crois que

je ne vaincrai jamais mes scrupules et je n'espère pas aussi
de surmonter l'inclination que j'ai pour vous. Elle me ren-
dra malheureuse et je me priverai de votre vue, quelque
violence qu'il m'en coûte. Je vous conjure, par tout le pouvoir que j'ai sur vous, de ne chercher aucune occasion de
me voir.

—I know that there is nothing harder than what I un-
dertake; I mistrust my own strength, supported by all my
arguments. What I think due to the memory of Monsieur
de Clèves would be ineffectual, if it were not reinforced
by my anxiety for my own peace of mind; and these arguments need to be strengthened by those of duty. But
though I mistrust myself, I think I shall never overcome
my scruples, and I do not hope to overcome my interest
in you. It will make me unhappy, and I shall deny myself
the pleasure of seeing you, whatever pain this may cost
me. (p. 152; translation, pp. 133–34)

Though she admits her love and the difficulty of overcoming
it, she uses this admission as an additional argument for her
course of action: to avoid seeing the man she loves at all costs.
It is quite clear from her emphatic speech and her circular argument that there is no way out.

The duke, having learned from what she has said, finally
understands her line of reasoning. What moments earlier he
called "fantôme de devoir" (her alleged duty to her husband),
he now understands to be a *personal* duty. He realizes that this
emphasis on the personal aggravates their situation, since
there are no ready-made arguments for defeating opinions
based on personal needs. The reader's attention is drawn to
this crucial discovery in the following passage, where M. de
Nemours supplies an interpretive reading of the situation.
Such emphasis on a central point is rhetorically significant in
that it guides the reader in his assessment of the principal

character's psychological makeup and prepares him for further developments in the story world:

—Il n'y a point d'obstacle, madame, reprit M. de Nemours. Vous *seule* vous opposez à mon bonheur; vous *seule* vous imposez une loi que la vertu et la raison ne vous sauraient imposer. (my italics)

—There is no obstacle, pleaded Monsieur de Nemours, you alone thwart my happiness, you alone impose a law which virtue and reason could not impose. (p. 152; translation, p. 134)

Her reasons and how she intends to enforce them are repeated once more, this time in summary fashion by the omniscient narrator. By repeating, a few pages from the end of the book, all the major points of her central argument as it was presented just three pages earlier, the narrator unequivocally gives the reader a final interpretive model for the novel. This is the last word about the princess's plight, and it is doubly authoritative, since it has come from two different voices (the character's and the narrator's):

Les raisons qu'elle avait de ne point épouser M. de Nemours lui paraissaient *fortes* du côté de son devoir et *insurmontables* du côté de son repos. La fin de l'amour de ce prince, et les maux de la jalousie qu'elle croyait infaillibles dans un mariage, lui montraient un malheur certain où elle s'allait jeter; mais elle voyait aussi qu'elle entreprenait une chose impossible, que de résister en présence au plus aimable homme du monde qu'elle aimait et dont elle était aimée, et de lui résister sur une chose qui ne choquait ni la vertu, ni la bienséance. Elle jugea que l'absence seule et l'éloignement pouvaient lui donner quelque force. (my italics)

Her reasons for not marrying Monsieur de Nemours seemed strong so far as her duty, and irrefutable so far as her tranquillity, was concerned. The fading of his love after marriage, and all the pangs of jealousy, which she regarded as certain, showed her the misery to which she would expose herself, but she saw too that she had assumed an impossible task in undertaking to resist the most fascinating of men, whom she loved and who loved her, in a matter which offended neither virtue nor propriety. She decided that only separation could give her strength. (pp. 155–56; translation, p. 136)

In describing her reasons for inner peace as "insurmountable" as opposed to the "strong" reasons for duty, the narrator emphatically recalls her principal motive, which is given further weight through the negative image of love in marriage. Then, in logical progression, the reader is reminded of the dichotomy between her reasoning and her feelings, awareness of which inevitably leads to retreat. The rest of the narrative confirms this final account of her reasoning and resolution: she withdraws from social life, enters a convent, and refuses to see the duke again. The novel is thus brought to its logical conclusion. We can accept this conclusion, even if our own view of love is different, since we have been led to it through narrative logic and emphasis, and through built-in interpretive readings. Such hermeneutic strategies reinforce the *effet de réel*, which, as Genette has shown, is not based on imitations of the real but is achieved instead through restrictions of the end goal.[30]

The novel's progressive focus on the personal needs of its central figure sets up a new kind of verisimilitude for the seventeenth-century public raised on conformity and respect for the norm. The text reinforces its own authority by exposing these conventions as untenable. The novel's shift in emphasis from public opinion to personal discoveries constitutes a claim

30. Genette, "Vraisemblance et motivation," pp. 17–18.

for a new order of belief.[31] That the depiction of such a new order met with considerable resistance at first is obvious from the initial responses to the book. Such evidence is proof of the fact that readers bring culturally conditioned frames of reference to their reading of novels. Mme. de La Fayette's seventeenth-century readers found it hard to accept Mme. de Clèves's exceptional conduct, since it challenged their society's foremost social code. *Bienséance*, defined by one authority as "non pas ce qui est honnête, mais ce qui convient aux personnes"[32] ("not what is honorable, but what is suitable to society"), is here rewritten as "bienséance, non pas ce qui convient aux personnes, mais ce qui me semble honnête" ("not what is suitable, but what seems to me to be honorable" [my translations]). Diametrically opposed to social convention, such a radical departure from the norm was not likely to be taken as *vraisemblable*. If, as Wolfgang Iser claims in *The Act of Reading*, the central function of literary texts is to make the reader aware of norms and conventions by questioning and negating those norms in order to encourage the reader to imagine something new, then *La Princesse de Clèves*, by rewriting *vraisemblance* and *bienséance*, is an excellent example of a fictional work that takes the reader of its time beyond habitual

31. Barbara Woshinsky has argued that, in this respect, *La Princesse de Clèves* is a forerunner of the eighteenth-century novel of sensibility. For instance, in discussing Mme. de Clèves, she writes, "For her, being true to oneself comes to mean being true to one's feelings, and personal morality depends on the fulfillment of an inner imperative. Thus she fuses morality and sensibility into a new, wholly subjective ethic" (*La Princesse de Clèves: The Tension of Elegance*, p. 111). The innovative nature of the novel is also central to Joan DeJean's discussion in "Lafayette's Ellipses: The Privileges of Anonymity" (*PMLA* 99 [1984]: 884–902); she argues that both Mme. de La Fayette's choice of anonymity and Mme. de Clèves's controversial conduct should be seen not as acts of avoidance but as affirmations, since both are instrumental in forging an *écriture féminine* (p. 887) and in bringing about a new type of reading of women's fiction (p. 885).

32. From Chapelain's *De la poésie représentative*, quoted and discussed by René Bray in *Formation de la doctrine classique*, p. 227.

frames of reference and, by doing so, makes for active reader response.[33]

To naturalize the unconventional and to make it believable, Mme. de La Fayette had to set up a coherent, authoritative narrative. She did so by closely joining the various frames of reference that shape our reading of this novel—the rhetorical, cultural, and historical. I have shown how narrative strategy makes the unusual more acceptable through the emphatic focus on the figural mind and its own coherent logic, and through references to history and cultural practice, which create a powerful *effet de réel*. The reaction to the novel by most of the author's contemporaries provides evidence of another sort of reading—that of the seventeenth-century reader who, instead of giving in to rhetorical manipulation, brought his own culturally conditioned response to the reading of the novel. More recently, Serge Doubrovsky, reading from a philosophic perspective, concluded that the only escape open to the Princesse de Clèves is suicide, while Nancy Miller, viewing the novel from a feminist perspective, offered a more positive interpretation by suggesting that Mme. de Clèves's renunciation of love may be seen as "a peculiarly feminine 'act of victory.' "[34] Still other readings are possible, as interests and ideologies change.[35]

Once we open the interpretive space between reader and

33. Iser, *The Act of Reading*, p. 208.

34. Serge Doubrovsky, "*La Princesse de Clèves*: une interprétation existentielle," *La Table Ronde*, no. 138 (1959): 48, and Nancy K. Miller, "Emphasis Added," p. 39. For another positive reading, from a feminist perspective, see Joan DeJean, "Lafayette's Ellipses."

35. German theories of reception (*Rezeptionsästhetik*) pay particular attention to the changing, culturally conditioned readings of literary works. A central concept that underlies a number of these theories is the "fusion of horizons" (drawn from Hans Georg Gadamer) and the related concept, "horizon of expectations." According to Karl Popper, the horizon of expectations plays the role of a frame of reference, without which experiences, observations, etc. would have no meaning" ("Naturgesetze und theoretische Systeme," in *Theorie und Realität*, ed. Hans Albert [Tübingen: Mohr, 1972], p. 49).

text, we also multiply the frames of reference that come into play. If we are aware of the complex frames of reference that enter into the production and reception of literary texts, then we can no longer agree with Roland Barthes's claim that "what goes on in a narrative is, from the referential (real) point of view, strictly *nothing*. What does 'happen' is language per se, the adventures of language, whose advent never ceases to be celebrated."[36] The problem of reference in narrative fiction is much more complex than Barthes would allow. It simply is not possible to confine the literary referent to words on a page. It must be studied on the level of the dialectic exchange between the reader and the text. If we keep this in mind, we realize the importance of the context of reading—a context made up of shifting frames of reference. It is these frames of reference that play the central role in a poetics of reading, since they help to account for different readings of the same text. In the case of *La Princesse de Clèves*, seventeenth-century readers, subject to strong conventional biases, resisted the novel's emphatic narrative strategies calculated to institute a new code of behavior. We get quite another reading if we imagine a reader, as I have done in this chapter, more open to rhetorical persuasion and less subject to the tyranny of convention.

36. Barthes, "An Introduction to the Structural Analysis of Narrative," *NLH* 6 (1975): 271. Translated from the original French version in *Communications* 8 (1966): 27.

T H R E E

Madame Bovary or the Dangers of Misreading

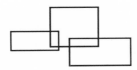

Ce qui me semble beau, ce que je voudrais faire, c'est un livre sur rien . . .
—FLAUBERT, *Correspondance*

Though the novel's title focuses the reader's attention on what he may well expect to be its central subject, such expectations are frustrated from the start, since the opening chapters focus on Charles, not Emma. Nor is this narrative focus a stable one, as soon becomes evident when other disconcerting hurdles are encountered. Through jarring contrasts and shifting perspectives, Flaubert's reader is soon drawn into a more active, hermeneutic reading; the central question is no longer "What will happen next?" but, rather, "Why are things told that way?" This heightened attention to narrative form takes us beyond the story world to a more global reading in which our central concern is no longer Emma's plight. Instead of wondering whether it is adultery that makes the novel go round,[1] or

1. According to Michael Riffaterre, the representations of the adulteress constitute the novel's central descriptive system and orient the reading process. Since the reader is familiar with this system and what it presupposes and entails, "presupposition offers an explanation, since it is by presupposing that a verbal sequence compels the reader to compare text and intertext" ("Flaubert's Presuppositions," *Diacritics* 11, [1981]: 5).

whether to feel sympathy or irony,[2] we begin to unveil not Emma but the narrator's discourse. Once we begin to see through his strategies, we begin to read within an expanded frame of reference. We are thus gradually initiated into a more open, critical reading while the narrator insistently draws our attention to form. Our awareness of language is further heightened when the narrator repeatedly illustrates the uses and abuses of language within the fictional world, and when he suddenly interpolates passages warning us about the manipulation and shortcomings of language, and the dangers of misreading.

By keeping the reader at a critical distance through various illusion-breaking devices, Flaubert's narrator works against verisimilitude. He destroys the *effet de réel* not only by undermining what is said and what happens in the story world, but also by going against the conventional form of the novel. Unlike *La Princesse de Clèves*, in which the narrator's redundant, one-directional discourse is at the service of verisimilitude, Flaubert's novel engages its readers in a multidirectional reading process.

Since the novel commands attention through its insistent irony and the disconcerting changes in the frames of reference set up by the narrative, my focus in this chapter will be on a rhetorical reading, presupposing a reader sensitive to style and narrative technique. While the text's rhetorical structures are the predominant framework for the discussion below, this focus does not preclude other frames of reference for reading *Madame Bovary*. I will briefly mention some of them, but dealing fully with the complex and multifaceted rhetorical analysis itself does not permit exploring them at length.

Right from the start of the novel there are a number of illu-

2. In *Flaubert: The Uses of Uncertainty* (Ithaca: Cornell University Press, 1974), p. 24off., Jonathan Culler makes the point that the reader of *Madame Bovary*, constantly vacillating between two opposing views of Emma, cannot settle on an either/or solution.

sion-breaking devices that catch the reader's attention and put him on his guard. The most remarkable departure from conventional storytelling is the narrator's refusal to set up a unified, coherent frame of reference for telling his story. Not only does the focus change after the first five chapters (from Charles to Emma), but so do the narrator's position and attitude. There are marked shifts from exterior surfaces to interior views, from sympathy to irony, and from first-person to third-person narration. Such infractions are striking, since one does not expect a narrator to change his position so radically vis-à-vis the story world or the reader. In doing so, he undermines the narrative project he himself set up.

Flaubert's narrator begins his tale by describing Charles from the point of view of a stranger. Charles, a new pupil, enters the classroom where everyone stares at him. His looks, dress, and demeanor are described, as well as the spectators' reaction to him. While the narrator, using the *nous* form, reveals himself as one of the pupils gaping at the stranger, his description does not conform to such a restricted vision.[3] The details he selects and his choice of language reveal that he is doing more than simply reporting what he witnessed. The most obvious example is the blown-up description of the boy's ridiculous cap, the depiction of which is a verbal tour de force that commands attention. Through the proliferation of details, the narrator takes the reader far beyond the field of vision and spontaneous reaction of a fellow classmate. Not only is it unlikely that anyone in such a situation would fix his attention

3. For an updated discussion of perspective or "focalization," see Gérard Genette, *Nouveau discours du récit*, pp. 49–50. According to Genette, focalization is, by definition, a restriction of the field of vision (p. 49). He distinguishes among three kinds: (1) zero focalization is described as variable perspective and/or as nonfocalization; (2) internal focalization gives the perspective of a character who is the center of all perception and thought; and (3) external focalization is situated at some point in the fictional world chosen by the narrator but outside of any particular character, thus excluding any possibility for inside views or thoughts (p. 50).

on one piece of clothing at the expense of missing the rest, but it is equally unlikely that anyone who had witnessed the scene would later recall the exact style and shape of the cap. That the narrator keeps the reader at a critical distance is apparent when he makes a negative remark regarding the hat, backed up by a devastating comparison: "une de ces pauvres choses, enfin, dont la laideur muette a des profondeurs d'expression comme le visage d'un imbécile"[4] ("one of those poor things, in fine, whose dumb ugliness has depths of expression, like an imbecile's face"). Instead of judging his character overtly, the narrator relies on the indirect technique of juxtaposing narrative and description, leaving it up to the reader to make the relevant connections. In a similar way, the same message is brought home once more a few lines later when Charles, whose naiveté and slowness are the cause of his classmates' repeated outbursts of laughter, is asked to copy the verb *ridiculus sum* twenty times—a punishment whose implications the reader cannot fail to note. Once familiar with Charles's limited resources, the reader cannot help but see the ironic situation and anticipate the ironic outcome when such different and incompatible people as Charles and Emma are brought together.[5]

That the narrator has considerably more knowledge than anyone who is merely a fellow classmate becomes even more obvious when, immediately following the classroom scene, he gives the family history of Charles's parents and an account of his upbringing and future studies, intrudes unexpectedly into his private thoughts and feelings, and provides a brief description of his first marriage. This kind of information is not com-

4. Flaubert, *Madame Bovary* (Paris: Garnier-Flammarion, 1966), p. 38. The English translation that follows is from Paul de Man, trans.; *Madame Bovary* (New York: W. W. Norton, 1965), p. 2. Hereafter, unless otherwise specified, page references to both these sources are given sequentially within parentheses. Parenthetical references to only one source are to the French edition.
5. For a distinction between the different kinds of irony—ranging from verbal to dramatic and situational—see Wayne Booth, *A Rhetoric of Irony*.

patible with the first-person narrative established in the beginning pages of the novel. Within a few pages of the first chapter the narrator thus flagrantly trespasses, going from the restricted field of vision he set up by encoding himself as one of the group to a more omniscient position.[6] Such drastic changes in perspective within the brief space of a short chapter are disconcerting, since they violate narrative logic. The reader is not merely confronted with alterations or modulations in perspective as Genette has claimed, but with a new modal system.[7] This is even more apparent when the narrator drops the *nous* form at the end of the first chapter, thereby removing himself from the field of action and giving himself carte blanche to be anywhere at any time. This change in narration from first to third person, combined with the change in perspective, sets up an entirely new "narrative situation."[8] Yet no sooner does the reader become used to this frame of narration than he is uprooted once more as his attention is shifted to Emma, who moves center stage beginning with chapter 6. By entering Emma's world, he is given a different frame of refer-

6. This is a case of what Genette has called "paralepsis," since the information given exceeds the narrative logic of the modal system in force. See his *Nouveau discours du récit*, p. 44, and "Discours du récit," p. 211.

7. See "Discours du récit," pp. 211–24, where Genette distinguishes between *altération* or modulations in perspective defined as momentary, isolated changes that do not disturb the overall coherence, since a dominant mode is maintained (p. 211), and *polymodalité*, characterized by the prevalence of different modes of focalization (p. 233). Though Genette discusses *Madame Bovary* under "alteration" (pp. 207–11) and contrasts it with the "polymodality" of *A la recherche du temps perdu*, I feel that the changes of perspective in Flaubert's novel are so radical and extensive that they do not merely "modulate" but set up an entirely new mode of narration.

8. For an updated discussion of what constitutes a "narrative situation," see Gérard Genette, *Nouveau discours du récit*, pp. 77–89. Genette charts the different narrative situations based on the combination of person and perspective (p. 83), and he concludes by expanding his chart, including the level of narration as well (p. 88). For a critique and rebuttal of some of Genette's revised views, see the lively exchange between Gérard Genette and Dorrit Cohn published in *Poétique* 61 (1985) under the title "Nouveaux nouveaux discours du récit" (pp. 101–109).

ence: the story world is now organized around her, and so is the narrator's discourse.

It is the treatment of Emma that makes us most aware of shifting perspectives. We first get an external, impartial description of her—the view of a stranger—as Charles visits her father's house for the first time: "Une jeune femme, en robe de mérinos bleu garnie de trois volants, vint sur le seuil de la maison pour recevoir M. Bovary, qu'elle fit entrer dans la cuisine" ("A young woman in a blue merino dress with three flounces came to the threshold of the door to receive Monsieur Bovary; she led him to the kitchen") (p. 48; translation, p. 10). Emma now enters the scene as a secondary character in Charles's world. Until chapter 6, we get only occasional glimpses of her—partly through Charles's and partly through the narrator's eyes, and through bits of reported speech—all of which we must piece together gradually to form a picture of her.[9] While most of chapter 5 centers on Charles, by describing his newly found happiness as Emma's husband, what is striking is the sudden juxtaposition of first Charles's, then Emma's, point of view about marriage in the chapter's final paragraphs. Three paragraphs from the end we are given a glimpse of Charles's most intimate thoughts through a passage of free indirect speech in which he briefly reviews his past life, asking himself when he could possibly have been this happy. The narrator brings these ruminations to a close by introducing a succinct, critical evaluation: "L'univers, pour lui, n'excédait pas le tour soyeux de son jupon" ("For him the universe did not extend beyond the silky circumference of her petticoat")

9. Jean Rousset's remark that the reader first sees Emma only through Charles needs qualification. Even in passages where the narrator specifies that it is Charles who is looking at Emma, the description is so complex that the reader suspects more than a single viewpoint. For example, the description of Emma's hand and hair (p. 49) points to a more experienced eye than Charles's in the critical appraisal of her beauty, while the use of technical terms (*phalanges*) betrays the interests and speech of the doctor. For Rousset's discussion see *Forme et signification* (Paris: Corti, 1964), pp. 114–17.

(p. 68; translation, p. 24). The sudden switch in perspective to Emma's disillusionment in the chapter's final paragraph stands in ironic contrast with the long account of Charles's conjugal bliss:

> Avant qu'elle se mariât, elle avait cru avoir de l'amour; mais le bonheur qui aurait dû résulter de cet amour n'étant pas venu, il fallait qu'elle se fût trompée, songeait-elle. Et Emma cherchait à savoir ce que l'on entendait au juste dans la vie par les mots de *félicité*, de *passion*, et d'*ivresse*, qui lui avaient paru si beaux dans les livres.

> Before marriage she thought herself in love; but since the happiness that should have followed failed to come, she must, she thought, have been mistaken. And Emma tried to find out what one meant exactly in life by the words *bliss, passion, ecstasy*, that had seemed to her so beautiful in books. (p. 69; translation, p. 24)

The abrupt juxtaposition, without any kind of transition, of Charles's and Emma's frames of mind emphasizes the difference in outlook and exemplifies stylistically what will be a way of life for them: they will live side by side, unable to communicate.[10]

This brief insight into Emma's illusions about romantic love, with its principal clichés conspicuously emphasized through the use of italics, provides the narrative link to the next chapter, which tells the reader about the books that have fed her imagination and that have encouraged her to view reality in terms of the fictions familiar to her. We now enter a new frame of reference, the world where Emma is the center of interest. She is the metonymic link through which Flaubert avoids total rupture. Yet, the reader remains puzzled by this striking break

10. The pattern has been set; all aspects of their life together show the same lack of communication, a fact the narrator will repeatedly underscore through narrative juxtaposition and stylistic contrast. See, for example, pp. 76, 222–23.

in the narrator's discourse, since the unexpected shift from one narrative frame to another is never explained. This interpretive gap makes for a more active reading while readers try to solve the puzzle.

It is significant that the chapter that draws us into Emma's universe is entirely devoted to one aspect of her background, her studies, and that among these the focus is almost exclusively on certain kinds of reading. We are made to view these readings from a critical distance, through the narrator's manipulation of point of view. It soon becomes apparent that we are seeing things neither through Emma's subjective vision nor from an impartial point of view. Though the center of vision remains unspecified, the narrator calls attention to the ironic handling of his subject through choice of detail, composition, and commentary. His critical attitude is quite obvious in the passage describing Emma's reading of Chateaubriand's *Génie du Christianisme*. There is a double thrust to his irony, directed not only at *what* Emma reads but also at *how* she reads. The passage's basic contrast is between the mock lyrical tone of the initial sentence—mimicking the emotional outbursts, flowing rhythm, and hyperbole of the kind of literature in question—and the long, critical analysis of Emma's reading habits that follows:

> Comme elle écouta, les premières fois, la lamentation sonore des mélancolies romantiques se répétant à tous les échos de la terre et de l'éternité! Si son enfance se fût écoulée dans l'arrière-boutique d'un quartier marchand, elle se serait peut-être ouverte alors aux envahissements lyriques de la nature, qui, d'ordinaire, ne nous arrivent que par la traduction des écrivains. Mais elle connaissait trop la campagne; elle savait le bêlement des troupeaux, les laitages, les charrues. Habituée aux aspects calmes, elle se tournait au contraire vers les accidentés. Elle n'aimait la mer qu'à cause de ses tempêtes, et la verdure

seulement lorsqu'elle était clairsemée parmi les ruines. Il fallait qu'elle pût retirer des choses une sorte de profit personnel; et elle rejetait comme inutile tout ce qui ne contribuait pas à la consommation immédiate de son coeur,— étant de tempérament plus sentimentale qu'artiste, cherchant des émotions et non des paysages.

How she listened at first to the sonorous lamentations of romantic melancholy re-echoing through the world and eternity! If her childhood had been spent in the shops of a busy city section, she might perhaps have opened her heart to those lyrical invasions of Nature, which usually come to us only through translation in books. But she knew the country too well; she knew the lowing of cattle, the milking, the ploughs. Accustomed to the quieter aspects of life, she turned instead to its tumultuous parts. She loved the sea only for the sake of its storms, and the green only when it was scattered among ruins. She had to gain some personal profit from things and she rejected as useless whatever did not contribute to the immediate satisfaction of her heart's desires—being of a temperament more sentimental than artistic, looking for emotions, not landscapes. (p. 71; translation, pp. 25–26)

The main attack is obviously on Emma's reading habits. Criticism is quite overt in the last sentence with its summary judgment of her attitude toward the world, a condemnation that is rendered more vivid through disparaging metaphors: "Il fallait qu'elle pût retirer des choses une sorte de *profit* personnel; et elle rejetait comme inutile tout ce qui ne contribuait pas à la *consommation* immédiate de son coeur" (my italics). This negative evaluation of Emma's reading habits is a clear indication that the narrator does more than simply give an account of her reading. The critical distance from which we are made to view her alerts us to the fact that there is more than meets the eye, which, in turn, encourages a more active reading where we fill in the blanks.

That the reader is to keep at a critical distance is equally obvious when the narrator describes the kinds of things Emma reads at the convent. A good example of his ironic undermining is the following description of the type of popular novel Emma consumes:

> Ce n'étaient qu'amours, amants, amantes, dames persécutées s'évanouissant dans des pavillons solitaires, postillons qu'on tue à tous les relais, chevaux qu'on crève à toutes les pages, forêts sombres, troubles du coeur, serments, sanglots, larmes et baisers, nacelles au clair de lune, rossignols dans les bosquets, *messieurs* braves comme des lions, doux comme des agneaux, vertueux comme on ne l'est pas, toujours bien mis, et qui pleurent comme des urnes.

> They were all about love, lovers, sweethearts, persecuted ladies fainting in lonely pavilions, postilions killed at every relay, horses ridden to death on every page, sombre forests, heart-aches, vows, sobs, tears and kisses, little boat-rides by moonlight, nightingales in shady groves, gentlemen brave as lions, gentle as lambs, virtuous as no one ever was, always well dressed, and weeping like fountains. (pp. 71–72; translation, p. 26)

The reader is kept alerted from the start through the brief put-down that precedes the parodic description of the kind of novel in question:[11] "Ce n'étaient qu'amours, amants, amantes." The narrator's intent, through the belittling *ne-que* structure, is obvious. That irony is at work is at once apparent when the initial critical remark is backed up by the long enu-

---

11. Linda Hutcheon's redefinition of parody as critical distance through irony (rather than through derision or mockery) may be applied to Flaubert's novel. See "Ironie et parodie: stratégie et structure," *Poétique* 36 (1978): 467–77.

meration of romantic clichés, most of them exaggerated for comic effect, followed by a series of equally banal and hyperbolic comparisons. The underlying ironic intent is flagrantly displayed when the narrator adds a comparison that debunks all the others: "vertueux comme on ne l'est pas" ("virtuous as no one ever was").

The narrator's critical reading of readings in this chapter not only provides clues about Emma's education and warns the reader about the limits of her *éducation sentimentale*, but also implies a more general evaluation of writing and reading. It makes us aware of language as fabrication, stressing the manipulatory powers both of texts and of readers. That the narrator looks unfavorably upon the appropriation of texts for personal gratification is made clear once more at the end of the chapter where he reminds the reader of Emma's selective, exploitative readings: "Cet esprit . . . qui avait aimé l'église pour ses fleurs, la musique pour les paroles de romances, et la littérature pour ses excitations passionnelles" ("This nature . . . that had loved the church for the sake of the flowers, and music for the words of the songs, and literature for the passions it excites" (p. 74; translation, p. 28).

Yet, there is more to it than that, something we gradually learn as we make our way through Flaubert's narrative. Not only does Emma's way of reading lend itself to pleasurable gratification, it also leads to dangerous delusions. This truth is brought home to the reader in the next chapter, and is repeated more than once before the end of the book. It is quite evident by the time we finish the novel that the repeated emphasis on Emma's way of reading serves as a negative model for the reader—a model not only for judging Emma and those around her, but also a model by which to evaluate our own reading of the very novel we are immersed in, and, by implication, of the world we live in. There is no explicit message to set the reader straight; meaning is to be inferred from striking contrasts and juxtapositions. It is no mere coincidence, for instance, that the first paragraph of the next chapter depicts Emma's reverie about the ideal honeymoon. This long passage, written almost entirely in free indirect discourse, gives the reader a close look at her way of thinking and feeling.[12] In switching to free indirect speech, the narrator is able to render Emma's consciousness by inscribing her own idiom and personal intonation into his discourse while maintaining third-person narration.[13] This merging of two voices sets up a complex, "dialogic" structure, at times combining speech characteristics of the character with traces of the narrator's style, which allows for subtle manipulation of point of view.[14] Through close proximity with the preceding chapter, the con-

12. For a detailed discussion of what has variously been called free indirect speech or discourse, *style* (or *discours*) *indirect libre*, or *erlebte Rede*, see Dorrit Cohn, *Transparent Minds*, pp. 99–140. Instead of using existing terminology, Cohn introduces the term "narrated monologue," since it holds a "mid-position between quoted monologue and psycho-narration, rendering the content of the figural mind more obliquely than the former, more directly than the latter" (p. 105). It is a method of "superimposing two voices that are kept distinct in the other two forms" (ibid.). Ann Banfield uses yet another term, "represented speech," in her article "The Formal Coherence of Represented Speech," *PTL* 3 (1978): 289–314.

13. By interpolating Emma's language into his own discourse, Flaubert's narrator creates a very special effect, which V. N. Vološinov has described as the dynamics of true verbal interaction (*Marxism and the Philosophy of Language*, trans. Ladislav Matejka and I. R. Titunik [New York and London: Seminar Press, 1973], p. 145). He sees in it "a completely *new*, positive tendency in active reception of another person's utterance, a *special direction* in which the dynamics of the interrelationship between reporting and reported speech moves" (p. 142). Cf. Dorrit Cohn's similar view, backed up by a grammatical explanation: "By employing the same basic tense for the narrator's *reporting language* and the character's *reflecting language*, two normally distinct linguistic currents are made to merge" (*Transparent Minds*, p. 103).

14. In *A Poetics of Composition*, trans. Valentina Zavarin and Susan Wittig (Berkeley: University of California Press, 1973), Boris Uspensky distinguishes between two kinds of free indirect speech, the "quasi direct discourse" in which the narrator's speech adopts speech characteristics of the character (p. 34ff.) and "narrated monologue" in which the character's reported speech or thoughts carry traces of the narrator's style or editing (p. 41ff.). Cf. Vološinov's discussion of "quasi-direct discourse" in *Marxism and the Philosophy of Language*, pp. 141–60.

nection between Emma's present desires and her past readings is obvious: she evaluates her own life against the background of what she has learned from texts. The imaginary
landscape of her wishful thinking is entirely made up of fictional commonplaces; it is as if the reader were being referred
back to the romantic clichés highlighted in the previous chapter, except that this time they are quoted in earnest, not from
an ironic distance, since the narrator does not intrude. The
change in perspective from the ironic account of Emma's studies given from a critical distance and the present uncensored
excursion into her intimate daydreams is striking:

> Elle songeait quelquefois que c'étaient là pourtant les
> plus beaux jours de sa vie, la lune de miel, comme on di-
> sait. Pour en goûter la douceur, il eût fallu, sans doute,
> s'en aller vers ces pays à noms sonores où les lendemains
> de mariage ont de plus suaves paresses! Dans des chaises
> de poste, sous des stores de soie bleue, on monte au pas
> des routes escarpées, écoutant la chanson du postillon,
> qui se répète dans la montagne avec les clochettes des
> chèvres et le bruit sourd de la cascade. Quand le soleil se
> couche, on respire au bord des golfes le parfum des ci-
> tronniers; puis, le soir, sur la terrasse des villas, seuls et
> les doigts confondus, on regarde les étoiles en faisant des
> projets. Il lui semblait que certains lieux sur la terre de-
> vaient produire du bonheur, comme une plante particu-
> lière au sol et qui pousse mal tout autre part. Que ne pou-
> vait-elle s'accouder sur le balcon des chalets suisses ou
> enfermer sa tristesse dans un cottage écossais, avec un
> mari vêtu d'un habit de velours noir à longues basques, et
> qui porte des bottes molles, un chapeau pointu et des
> manchettes!

She thought, sometimes, that, after all, this was the
happiest time of her life: the honeymoon, as people called
it. To taste the full sweetness of it, it would no doubt have

been necessary to fly to those lands with sonorous names where the days after marriage are full of the most suave laziness! In post-chaises behind blue silken curtains, one rides slowly up steep roads, listening to the song of the postilion re-echoed by the mountains, along with the bells of goats and the muffled sound of a waterfall. At sunset on the shores of gulfs one breathes in the perfume of lemon-trees; then in the evening on the villa-terraces above, one looks hand in hand at the stars, making plans for the future. It seemed to her that certain places on earth must bring happiness, as a plant peculiar to the soil, and that cannot thrive elsewhere. Why could not she lean over balconies in Swiss châlets, or enshrine her melancholy in a Scotch cottage, with a husband dressed in a black velvet coat with long tails, and thin shoes, a pointed hat and frills? (p. 75; translation, pp. 28–29)

It is by now quite obvious that irony—verbal, situational, and dramatic—is one of the narrator's principal resources for telling his tale and coaching the reader. It structures our reading and guides our interpretation, encouraging us to go beyond a simple, literal reading. In the present instance, for example, we do not simply take Emma's daydream at face value but infer other layers of meaning. When we read this passage against the background of the previous chapter, it becomes immediately apparent that her expectations grow directly out of the world of fiction. If we consider her reverie in the larger context of all we have read so far, another meaning emerges: knowing what we know about Charles's education and personality, now viewed in contrast with Emma's, we cannot help but perceive the ironic situation of a couple totally unsuited for each other. Once we see this, we participate in dramatic irony: both narrator and reader know more than the characters, are able to view them from a critical distance, and anticipate their fate. By thus allowing us to read between the lines and to participate in the writing of the plot, the narrator gets us more actively involved in his narrative project.[15]

Through additional contrastive descriptions, the narrator keeps reminding his readers how incompatible Charles and Emma are. A few paragraphs after her reverie, the juxtaposition—in two successive paragraphs—of Charles's shortcomings and Emma's image of the ideal man stand in ironic contrast. The narrator stresses this contrast by incorporating parts of the characters' speech in his own discourse—first in a statement by Charles rendered in indirect speech and conspicuously set off by *disait-il*, then in a whole passage in free indirect discourse, thus allowing direct insight into Emma's way of thinking:

> La conversation de Charles était plate comme un trottoir de rue, et les idées de tout le monde y défilaient, dans leur costume ordinaire, sans exciter d'émotion, de rire ou de rêverie. Il n'avait jamais été curieux, disait-il, pendant qu'il habitait Rouen, d'aller voir au théâtre les acteurs de Paris. Il ne savait ni nager, ni faire des armes, ni tirer le pistolet, et il ne put, un jour, lui expliquer un terme d'équitation qu'elle avait rencontré dans un roman.
>
> Un homme, au contraire, ne devait-il pas tout connaître, exceller en des activités multiples, vous initier aux énergies de la passion, aux raffinements de la vie, à tous

15. For a discussion of the reader's active participation, through reconstruction, in the ironic text, see Wayne Booth, *A Rhetoric of Irony*. See also Wolfgang Iser, *The Act of Reading*, for a discussion of how the reader's construction of the text ("acts of constitution") is stimulated by the structure of the blank (pp. 180–203). Both authors include a discussion of the emotional response to such structures of reading: Booth emphasizes the added pleasure the reader experiences when invited to share the narrator's superior position, while Iser claims that the reader's active participation while filling in the blanks gives him the illusion of being involved in something "real." By thus closely linking textual features, structures of reading, and affective response, they give excellent examples for studying how the various frames of reference are related and intersect.

les mystères? Mais il n'enseignait rien, celui-là, ne savait rien, ne souhaitait rien. Il la croyait heureuse; et elle lui en voulait de ce calme si bien assis, de cette pesanteur sereine, du bonheur même qu'elle lui donnait.

Charles's conversation was commonplace as a street pavement, and every one's ideas trooped through it in their everyday garb, without exciting emotion, laughter, or thought. He had never had the curiosity, he said, while he lived at Rouen, to go to the theatre to see the actors from Paris. He could neither swim, nor fence, nor shoot, and one day he could not explain some term of horsemanship to her that she had come across in a novel.

A man, on the contrary, should he not know everything, excel in manifold activities, initiate you into the energies of passion, the refinements of life, all mysteries? But this one taught nothing, knew nothing, wished nothing. He thought her happy, and she resented this easy calm, this serene heaviness, the very happiness she gave him. (p. 76; translation, p. 29)

The discrepancy between Emma's imaginary ideal and stark reality is ironically highlighted when the narrator introduces pejorative figurative language to describe Charles's conversation as "plate comme un trottoir de rue," and when he draws attention to the nullity of Charles's ideas through personification ("les idées de tout le monde y défilaient, dans leur costume ordinaire"). It comes as no surprise to the reader when three pages later a disillusioned Emma repeats to herself, "Pourquoi, mon Dieu, me suis-je mariée?"[16] ("Why, for Heaven's sake, did I marry?") (p. 79; translation, p. 31).

16. The narrator keeps reminding the reader of their incompatibility through further contrastive description. One of the most memorable reminders is the passage in which the narrator first takes a close look at Charles's nighttime reveries, followed in the next paragraph by Emma's. The contrast is striking: while Charles thinks about their daughter growing up, Emma imagines herself eloping with her lover in a romantic setting (pp. 222–24).

Though we could easily condemn Emma's conclusion as one-sided, given her biased "reading" of life based on the literature that has informed her, the narrator constantly pushes us beyond such easy solutions.[17] For one thing, he repeatedly stresses the ironic situation in which she finds herself—including her marriage to an unsuitable mate and the crassness and banality that surround her. For another, he comes back to the problem of reading more than once, devoting a long passage to it at the end of part 2 while describing Emma's experience at the opera (pp. 248–51) during a performance of *Lucia di Lammermoor*. The detailed description of this experience, backed up by references to previous passages and the narrator's commentary, stands out in the text and commands the reader's attention.

The passage begins with an explicit reference to Emma's schoolgirl readings, explaining the effect they still have on her: "Elle se retrouvait dans les lectures de la jeunesse, en plein Walter Scott. Il lui semblait entendre, à travers le brouillard, le son des cornemuses écossaises se répéter sur les bruyères. D'ailleurs, le souvenir du roman facilitant l'intelligence du libretto, elle suivait l'intrigue phrase à phrase"[18] ("She felt herself carried back to the reading of her youth, into the midst of Walter Scott. She seemed to hear through the mist the sound of the Scotch bagpipes re-echoing over the moors. Her remembrance of the novel helping her to understand the libretto, she followed the story phrase by phrase") (p. 248; translation, p. 161). The repeated mention of Emma's early readings is signif-

17. Nonetheless, a reader less attentive to the text's rhetorical strategies or unfamiliar with the social and economic conditions of the time might grow impatient with Flaubert's heroine. For instance, students of mine, judging her by today's standards, have wondered why Emma fails to do something to get herself out of her oppressive situation. They were unable to understand her because it did not occur to them to evaluate her behavior within the proper cultural and historical frame of reference.

18. See part 1, chapter 6, for the first reference to Emma's reading of Walter Scott.

icant not only because of the narrator's insistence on their last-ing influence, but also because, in the present instance, he studies their effect in relation to her own experience of love. It is the close attention the narrator pays to the joint influence of art and life and how this shapes Emma's reaction to *Lucia di Lammermoor* that is of central importance. This double focus gives us new insight into the complexity of reading, which we recognize by now as one of the novel's leading themes.[19]

It is significant that we have just been told in the preceding chapter about Emma's great suffering and prolonged illness following Rodolphe's betrayal. It is ironic that despite her dis-astrous experience with love, Emma is carried away once more to the heights of illusion while listening to the opera. The nar-rator shows us how this happens by focusing on her growing empathy. At the same time, he keeps us at a critical distance by introducing a number of disparaging analogies that stand in ironic contrast with Emma's spontaneous reaction. For in-stance, in the following description of Emma's growing em-pathy for the heroine, he undermines her enthusiasm by intro-ducing a dissonant comparison: "Elle s'emplissait le coeur de ces lamentations mélodieuses qui se trainaient à l'accom-pagnement des contrebasses, comme des cris de naufragés dans le tumulte d'une tempête" ("Her heart filled with these melodious lamentations that were accompanied by the lugu-brious moanings of the doublebases, like the cries of the drowning in the tumult of a tempest") (p. 249; translation, p. 162).

From the description of Emma's experience of empathy the reader learns that it is based on a comparison between her life and the heroine's, a process of identification that highlights both similarity and difference:[20]

19. For the repeated emphasis on reading, see pp. 70–74, 92, 116–18, 191, 223, 240, 248–51, 260–61, 281, 289, 306, 310, 312, 346.
20. For a discussion of the role of empathy in the reading process, see Anselm

Elle reconnaissait tous les enivrements et les angoisses dont elle avait manqué mourir. La voix de la chanteuse ne lui semblait être que le retentissement de sa conscience, et cette illusion qui la charmait quelque chose même de sa vie. Mais personne sur la terre ne l'avait aimée d'un pareil amour.

She recognised all the intoxication and the anguish that had brought her close to death. The voice of the prima donna seemed to echo her own conscience, and the whole fictional story seemed to capture something of her own life. But no one on earth had loved her with such love. (p. 249; translation, p. 162)

While Emma gets carried away by what the narrator explicitly calls "illusion," the reader is kept at a distance; instead of a close description of the passionate parting scene, he is given a brief summary that is nothing but a string of romantic clichés: "Les amoureux parlaient des fleurs de leur tombe, de serments, d'exil, de fatalité, d'espérances, et, quand ils poussèrent l'adieu final, Emma jeta un cri aigu, qui se confondit avec la vibration des derniers accords" ("The lovers spoke of the flowers on their tomb, of vows, exile, fate, hopes; and when they uttered the final farewell, Emma gave a sharp cry that mingled with the vibrations of the last chords") (p. 249; translation, p. 162).

The narrator's real tour de force comes when he momentarily allows Emma to view her life in ironic contrast with the romantic heroine's. In a moment of unexpected insight, she presents a negative reading not only of her life but also of the deceptive power of art. Double irony is at work here: Emma's self-irony and "narrative" irony, as the narrator allows the one character whose misreadings he has repeatedly highlighted to do a critical reading. It is a long passage almost entirely writ-

Haverkamp, "Illusion und Empathie." For a brief discussion of this view of reading, see above, Chapter One, pp. 9–10.

ten in free indirect discourse, which shifts the reader's attention to Emma's mind while the narrator remains in the background. Emma begins by comparing her life to Lucia's. After
briefly recalling her wedding day, the contrast between the fictional situation and her own prompts her to look at her life
critically, to ask a leading question and to think wishfully
about another kind of life:

> Pourquoi donc n'avait-elle pas, comme celle-là, résisté,
> supplié? Elle était joyeuse, au contraire, sans s'apercevoir
> de l'abîme où elle se précipitait . . . Ah! si, dans la fraî-
> cheur de sa beauté, avant les souillures du mariage et la
> désillusion de l'adultère, elle avait pu placer sa vie sur
> quelque grand coeur solide, alors la vertu, la tendresse,
> les voluptés et le devoir se confondant, jamais elle ne se-
> rait descendue d'une félicité si haute.

> Why didn't she, like this woman, resist and implore? In-
> stead, she had walked joyously and unwittingly towards
> the abyss . . . Ah! if in the freshness of her beauty, before
> the degradation of marriage and the disillusions of adul-
> tery, she could have anchored her life upon some great,
> strong heart! Virtue, affection, sensuous pleasure and
> duty would have combined to give her eternal bliss. (p.
> 250; translation, p. 162)

Instead of being carried away, as usual, by the illusion-making
power of her wishful thinking, Emma stops short this time
and instead looks critically at both the life of passion and its
representation in art:

> Mais ce bonheur-là, sans doute, était un mensonge ima-
> giné pour le désespoir de tout désir. Elle connaissait à pré-
> sent la petitesse des passions que l'art exagérait. S'effor-
> çant donc d'en détourner sa pensée, Emma voulait ne
> plus voir dans cette reproduction de ses douleurs qu'une
> fantaisie plastique bonne à amuser les yeux.

But such happiness, she realized, was a lie, a mockery to taunt desire. She knew now how small the passions were that art magnified. So, striving for detachment, Emma resolved to see in this reproduction of her sorrows a mere formal fiction for the entertainment of the eye. (p. 250; translation, pp. 162–63)

Yet, irony upon irony, this momentary resolve is not put into practice, since a moment later (in the very next paragraph) we see Emma fall prey once more to the illusion-building powers of art while she imagines a love affair with the leading tenor. The narrator calls attention to this ironic reversal by explaining how this illusion comes about, after first reminding us of Emma's critical attitude: "Toutes ses velléités de dénigrement s'évanouissaient sous la poésie du rôle qui l'envahissait, et, entraînée vers l'homme par l'illusion du personage, elle tâcha de se figurer sa vie, cette vie retentissante, extraordinaire, splendide, et qu'elle aurait pu mener, cependant, si le hasard l'avait voulu" ("All her attempts at critical detachment were swept away by the poetic power of the acting, and, drawn to the man by the illusion of the part, she tried to imagine his life—extraordinary, magnificent, notorious, the life that could have been hers if fate had willed it") (p. 251; translation, p. 163). The end of the sentence takes us back to Emma's internal vision as the narrator's discourse subtly changes from objective statement to free indirect speech. What follows is a long reverie during which Emma imagines herself as the singer's mistress, traveling with him from city to city. We are kept from empathizing with Emma, not only because the narrator's ironic portrait of the tenor—whom he describes a few paragraphs earlier as an opportunist, a heartbreaker, and a mediocre artist—keeps us at a safe distance, but also because the disparaging description of the passions represented on stage reveals the narrator's ironic intent: "Ils étaient tous sur la même ligne à gesticuler; et la colère, la vengeance, la jalousie, la terreur, la miséricorde et la stupéfaction s'exhalaient à la fois de leurs bouches entr'ouvertes" ("They were lined up in one single gesticulating row, breathing forth anger, vengeance, jealousy, terror, mercy and surprise all at once from their open mouths") (p. 251; translation, p. 163).

How is this long passage on reading to be interpreted? Once again, there is no single, simple answer. We could concur with the narrator's earlier judgment of Emma's reading habits and see the present instance as one more example of how she appropriates art for personal gratification. We could also see it as another illustration of how easily Emma falls prey to illusions. Yet the detailed description of empathy has taught us that there is more to it than that. We have seen Emma subject herself to a complex process of identification during which she compared life and art—a process that led her to critical insight. Now, is it human or merely Emma's folly to be carried away by new illusions? Though we may not be sure what the final verdict on Emma's illusions will be, as Flaubert's readers we are constantly kept from having such illusions. By keeping us at a critical distance, the narrator checks our emotions and freezes our illusions. We are not allowed to get carried away by affect: there are no satisfying imaginary trips or *excitations passionnelles* for the reader of *Madame Bovary*! We are thus denied the pleasure of emotional involvement but are given instead the intellectual pleasure of sharing the narrator's superior position from which all is viewed critically. Yet even from this lofty position, there are no simple, unobstructed views. We must withhold judgment and see what else there is.

If the above passage is read within the context of the novel as a whole, we realize that Emma is not the primary target. In one of the novel's rare straightforward passages, the narrator, in an almost lyrical voice, reflects upon the universal shortcomings of language. This passage grows out of a critique of Rodolphe who, unlike Emma, recognizes romantic clichés for what they are but misinterprets nonetheless. His misreadings stand in ironic contrast with Emma's: while she believes in the existence of true passion behind all those clichés, he, aware of the use of stereotypes, fails to see that they may be used, *faute de mieux*, to express real feelings. That the blasé lover is wrong to dismiss Emma's love talk as one more instance of what he sees as "l'éternelle monotonie de la passion, qui a toujours les mêmes formes et le même langage" ("the eternal monotony of passion, that has always the same shape and the same language") is obvious when the narrator interpolates a long critique of this way of thinking while advancing his own view of language:

> Il ne distinguait pas, cet homme si plein de pratique, la dissemblance des sentiments sous la parité des expressions. Parce que des lèvres libertines ou vénales lui avaient murmuré des phrases pareilles, il ne croyait que faiblement à la candeur de celles-là; on en devait rabattre, pensait-il, les discours exagérés cachant les affections médiocres; comme si la plénitude de l'âme ne débordait pas quelquefois par les métaphores les plus vides, puisque personne, jamais, ne peut donner l'exacte mesure de ses besoins, ni de ses conceptions, ni de ses douleurs, et que la parole humaine est comme un chaudron fêlé où nous battons des mélodies à faire danser les ours, quand on voudrait attendrir les étoiles.

> He was unable to see, this man so full of experience, the variety of feelings hidden within the same expressions. Since libertine or venal lips had murmured similar phrases, he only faintly believed in the candor of Emma's; he thought one should beware of exaggerated declarations which only serve to cloak a tepid love; as though the abundance of one's soul did not sometimes overflow with empty metaphors, since no one ever has been able to give the exact measure of his needs, his concepts, or his sorrows. The human tongue is like a cracked cauldron on

which we beat out tunes to set a bear dancing when we
would make the stars weep with our melodies. (p. 219;
translation, p. 138)

This passage is exceptional in its opinionated, straightforward
pronouncement. It stands out in the novel and is a key passage for the reader.[21] It warns him about the shortcomings of
language and the dangers of misreading. The havoc this creates in people's lives is obvious when Rodolphe lightly dismisses Emma's love.

Though the present passage is unique in its indictment of
language, the narrator has other means to get the same message across. Through narrative form, we are progressively
made aware of a more global reading that takes us beyond Emma's plight. A striking example is another switch in narrative
focus in the first chapter of part 2, which begins with the description of Yonville l'Abbaye, the provincial town to which
the Bovarys are moving to improve their situation. This description is far from innocent: it is neither a neutral background description to help situate the couple in their new milieu nor a description of their point of view as they arrive in
the new place—either one of which would have been in keeping with narrative logic and economy. Instead, we are presented with a highly selective, evaluative description of the
town and its surrounding countryside—not an impartial, pan-
oramic view from lofty heights, but a biased view from an
ironic distance. This ironic mode is communicated through the
almost exclusive focus on negative aspects of the place, backed

21. The narrator intrudes with another statement about language while describing the sentimental life of Emma and Léon: "D'ailleurs, la parole est un
laminoir qui allonge toujours les sentiments" ("Besides, speech is like a rolling
machine that always stretches the sentiment it expresses") (p. 260; translation,
p. 169). Cf. a similar statement in which the narrator speaks of the "envahisse-
ments lyriques de la nature, qui, d'ordinaire, ne nous arrivent que par la tra-
duction des écrivains" ("lyrical invasions of Nature, which usually come to us
only through translation in books") (p. 71; translation, p. 25).

up by a series of derogatory expressions and disparaging analogies. This excess of information through the steady focus on negative detail puts us on our guard. We begin to suspect that topographic and architectural details exceed the simple, direct reference from signifier to signified and gradually add up to another frame of reference where significance must be inferred.

One thing we infer when we read this description within the framework of Emma's story is that she will find this place unbearable, that she will find herself once more in an ironic situation. How could she, given her romantic imagination, be happy in a setting described as a *contrée bâtarde* (mongrel land), *paysage sans caractère* (landscape without character), and *bourg paresseux* (lazy village), a place that looks like "un gardien de vaches qui fait la sieste au bord de l'eau" ("a cowherd taking a nap by the side of the river") (p. 106; translations, pp. 49–50). Nor will she find anything of interest in the poorly furnished church that has no organ, whose wood is rotting and that displays a sculpture of the Virgin Mary that is obviously in bad taste, "vêtue d'une robe de satin, coiffée d'un voile de tulle semé d'étoiles d'argent, et toute empourprée aux pommettes comme une idole des îles Sandwich" ("clothed in satin, wearing a tulle veil sprinkled with silver stars and with cheeks stained red like an idol of the Sandwich Islands") (p. 107; translation, p. 50). We are given an equally ironic view of the city hall when our attention is turned toward the ridiculous "coq gaulois, appuyé d'une patte sur la Charte et tenant de l'autre les balances de la justice" ("Gallic cock, resting one foot upon the Charter and holding in the other the scales of Justice") (p. 107; translation, p. 51). Such descriptive details definitely have a narrative function: they predict a negative turn of events for the principal story.[22]

22. Roland Barthes has another view of the function of descriptive details, playing down their predictive function while stressing the role they play in creating the *effet de réel*. See his "L'Effet de réel," pp. 84–89. Mieke Bal, on the

Yet there is more. Additional meaning can gradually be inferred as we progress in our reading but can only be assessed fully in a retrospective reading of the novel. Once we take a more global view of this chapter, we see the significance of the particular emphasis given the pharmacist Homais in this initial description of the town's inhabitants. That he is someone who likes to stand out is evident from the detailed description of his pharmacy, to which the reader's attention is drawn through the introductory statement, "Mais ce qui attire le plus les yeux, c'est, en face de l'auberge du *Lion d'or*, la pharmacie de M. Homais!" ("But what catches the eye most of all is Mr. Homais' pharmacy, right across from the Lion d'Or") (p. 107; translation, p. 51). The man's *amour-propre* is highlighted when the narrator points out that the pharmacist's name is displayed twice in golden letters—on an enormous sign that stretches across the entire store front, and once more on a smaller but equally striking sign inside the pharmacy (pp. 107–108). When the reader is introduced to the first citizens of Yonville gathered at the inn, it is Homais who dominates the conversation. What is remarkable from now on are the long, direct quotations of character-speech, giving us intimate knowledge of how the various villagers think and speak. Thus a wide range of social discourse is woven into the narrative fabric.

The narrator's emphasis on social speech does not go unnoticed. It is not there merely to advance the story and to give it local color and a good dosage of the expected *effet de réel* but, most importantly, to gradually create an indictment of language, of its uses and abuses. Such a negative reading of social speech is implicit in the repeated ironic interplay between the narrator's discourse and the characters' speech, as well as between different kinds of character-speech. The most obvious

---

other hand, argues against Barthes's position by emphasizing the diegetic function of details in *Madame Bovary*. See her *Narratologie*, pp. 89–109.

example is the chapter devoted to the country fair in which the narrator mischievously undercuts both the speeches given by the various dignitaries and the love talk between Emma and Rodolphe; he switches back and forth from one to the other, thus abruptly juxtaposing passages of disparate speech, a procedure that produces a highly comic effect.

In the chorus of social voices it is Homais's voice that stands out. He dominates conversations, has something to say about everything, and is the only one in Yonville who has an insatiable desire to see himself in print. His outlandish ideas and exaggerated style reach beyond the borders of his town, since he regularly contributes articles to the newspaper in Rouen and sends off monographs on such diverse and trivial topics as *Statistique générale du canton d'Yonville, suivie d'observations climatologiques* and *Du cidre, de sa fabrication et de ses effets*.[23]

In this polyphonic novel of intersecting voices there is none of the fruitful cross-pollination of the dialogic extolled by Bakhtin and his followers.[24] Instead, the various discourses are deconstructed through irony, shown to be self-enclosed, sterile, and destructive in as far as they affect the way people think, feel, and act. Yet the reader finds himself in a privileged position, since while he is immersed in the patchwork of social discourses, he also witnesses the deconstruction of the stereotypes through narrative technique. The narrator thus shows us that language is not merely a power that controls us, but

23. The narrator's ironic handling of Homais's writing is obvious from the long quotations of his newspaper articles: his convoluted style and distorted accounts of events stand in ironic contrast with the narrator's crisp style and his version of the same events. A telling example is Homais's untruthful, bombastic description of the country fair in the *Fanal de Rouen*, which sharply contrasts with the narrator's account of the fair (pp. 182–83). For other passages of Homais's ironic portrayal, see pp. 107–109, 121, 158, 165, 210, 302.

24. For Bakhtin's conception of the novel, see *The Dialogic Imagination*, ed. Michael Holquist (Austin: University of Texas Press, 1981). See also V. N. Vološinov, *Marxism and the Philosophy of Language*, pp. 142–46, and Tzvetan Todorov, *Mikhaïl Bakhtine: le principe dialogique*, which includes "Écrits du Cercle de Bakhtine" (Paris: Seuil, 1981).

that we have the power to manipulate it—as he does through irony and jarring contrasts.

As we make our way through this indictment of language, we realize that although the focus—after chapter 5—is primarily on Emma, she is not the narrator's primary target. This becomes clear as her way of thinking and speaking is pitched against the speech of others, including the speech of clergymen, doctors, and various townspeople, among whom Homais stands out. It is his speech and the havoc he creates that receive the full ironic thrust. This is obvious when the novel's ending is seen in relation to the novel as a whole. It is significant that the pharmacist has the last word. Instead of closing the novel at its most dramatic moment, Emma's gruesome death, the narrator adds three anticlimactic chapters. The focus shifts first to a "philosophical" discussion between the priest and the pharmacist during the wake—another instance of the ironic interplay of social voices—to a close account of Charles's misfortunes (we begin to suspect that the novel may end the way it began, with the focus on Charles), and finally to a close-up of Homais in the last few pages of the novel. By the time we read the last paragraph, there is no doubt as to the narrator's final intention: to unveil Homais and, through him, the destructive potential of language. It is now clear that through speaking and writing, the pharmacist has impressed the gullible villagers, who take his rhetoric for superior knowledge, consulting him rather than Bovary when needing medical help. Equally gullible are the authorities who reward him for his questionable writings and unabashed self-promotion.

The narrator has led us to this critical view of Homais by disclosing his secret ambition (the *croix d'honneur*), and by undermining his attempts at self-promotion through ironic counterpoint.[25] Finally, there is a damning summary of Homais's

25. For instance, Homais's claim, "Je suis membre de plusieurs sociétés savantes" ("I am a member of several learned societies"), is immediately coun-

activities in which irony gives way to direct attack: "Alors Homais inclinait vers le Pouvoir. Il rendit secrètement à M. le Préfet de grands services dans les élections. Il se vendit, enfin, il se prostitua" ("Homais' next step was trying to win over the Government to his cause. He secretly did the prefect several favors during the elections. He sold, in a word, prostituted himself") (p. 364; translation, p. 253). By calling him a "prostitute," the narrator unveils Homais—not Emma, the adulteress—as the novel's ultimate culprit, the epitome of moral corruption.[26]

Read against the background of this indictment, the novel's final paragraphs, coming immediately after the melodramatic account of Charles's misfortunes, acquire their full meaning:

> Depuis la mort de Bovary, trois médecins se sont succédé à Yonville sans pouvoir y réussir, tant M. Homais les a tout de suite battus en brèche. Il fait une clientèle d'enfer; l'autorité le ménage et l'opinion publique le protège.
>
> Il vient de recevoir la croix d'honneur.

> Since Bovary's death three doctors have succeeded one another in Yonville without any success, so effectively did Homais hasten to eradicate them. He has more customers than there are sinners in hell; the authorities treat him kindly and he has the public on his side.

---

tered by the narrator's correction, "Il l'était d'une seule" ("He was a member of a single one") (p. 364; translation, p. 253).

26. Though the narrator also uses the word "prostitution" in reference to Emma when she decides, at the height of her financial ruin, to turn to Rodolphe for help, he stresses that she is not aware of what she is doing (whereas Homais sells himself knowingly): "Elle partit donc vers la Huchette, sans s'apercevoir qu'elle courait s'offrir à ce qui l'avait tantôt si fort exaspérée, ni se douter le moins du monde de cette prostitution" ("So she set out towards La Huchette, unaware that she was hastening to offer what had so angered her a while ago, not in the least conscious of her prostitution") (p. 328; translation, p. 225).

He has just been given the cross of the Legion of Honor.
(p. 366; translation, p. 255)

The explicit revelation of Homais's professional abuses in the next-to-the-last paragraph, ironically followed by the brief statement of his success—conspicuously set off as a single, concluding paragraph—is the final clue. By allowing a charlatan to triumph after repeatedly undermining all he says and does, the narrator brings the novel to an ironic closure that invites active reader response. Such is the novel's last word— a word whose full meaning emerges only when we measure it against other textual elements and the various vantage points through which the narrator's shifting position has taken us. Though there is no simple interpretive closure, the final paragraphs are a powerful indictment that helps us put the multiple frames of reference into place.

The reader is now in a position to revise his view of Emma's situation. In a retrospective reading, she is bound to get more sympathy once the reader has taken a closer look at the people who surround her and has been given insight into the problematic nature of language. The central question is not, as Jonathan Culler has argued, "Is she foolish woman made tragic heroine or tragic heroine revealed as foolish woman?"[27] Though his answer is *both*, and he rightly cautions against falling into the narrow reading of *either/or*, the novel's range is still broader than that and goes beyond such considerations of Emma's image.[28] Flaubert's narrator has done more than merely switch back and forth from sympathy to irony, or "simply observe Emma from every angle that he possibly could";[29]

27. Culler, *Flaubert: The Uses of Uncertainty*, p. 140.
28. An argument for a broader reading was made by D. G. Charleton when he reviewed Culler's book in *TLS* (6 December 1974, p. 1391) under the title "The Language of Disorder."
29. This observation was made by Louis Auchincloss in a short piece that appeared in the *New York Times Book Review* entitled "Flaubert and James—Opposing Points of View" (24 June 1984).

he has also provided insight into more than one center of perception and has juggled contrastive points of view that take
the reader beyond her plight.

While this rhetorical reading has enabled me to emphasize
how various narrative strategies converge to guide the reader,
it does not preclude other readings of the novel. For instance,
if we were to read *Madame Bovary* from the perspective of current theories of reception describing reading as appropriation,
identification, or self-exploration, then we might not be in-
clined to accept the narrator's ironic view of Emma's reading
habits. By setting up an alternate frame of reference for viewing them, we could choose and emphasize those passages that
are in harmony with the theory under consideration. For example, to show how fictions have the power to enhance experience, we could single out the following passage in which
Emma draws an analogy between her own situation (having
just fallen in love) and similar situations experienced by her
most cherished fictional heroines:

> Alors elle se rappela les héroïnes des livres qu'elle avait
> lus, et la légion lyrique de ces femmes adultères se mit à
> chanter dans sa mémoire avec des voix de soeurs qui la
> charmaient. Elle devenait elle-même comme une partie
> véritable de ces imaginations et réalisait la longue rêverie
> de sa jeunesse, en se considérant dans ce type d'amou-
> reuse qu'elle avait tant envié.

> Then she recalled the heroines of the books that she had
> read, and the lyric legion of these adulterous women be-
> gin to sing in her memory with the voice of sisters that
> charmed her. She became herself, as it were, an actual
> part of these lyrical imaginings; at long last, as she saw
> herself among those lovers she had so envied, she ful-
> filled the love-dream of her youth. (p. 191; translation, p.
> 117)

Novels could thus be viewed positively as models for interpreting experience. Yet in so viewing them, we would obviously enter into direct conflict with the narrator's rhetorical design and with the ironic underpinnings of this passage.

Another alternative would be to graft a deconstructive reading onto the rhetorical one. This could easily be done, not only because Flaubert's narrator calls attention to all kinds of misreading and gives more than one model for deconstructing language, but also because a basic paradox underlies the novel: although the narrator teaches us to mistrust language, he also shows, through the force of his own rhetorical skills, how language can be used toward constructive ends. But there is no telling, once we have been led to mistrust language, when this mistrust may undermine the narrator's own authority.

My aim, however, is not to deconstruct the narrator's discourse by showing how it undermines its own philosophy; nor do I intend to show how the text's philosophy may undermine our reading. My point is that a poetics of reading built on the concept of multiple systems of reference does not put us in a position where we have to choose one of the readings over another (the either/or approach) but, rather, that it enables us to see which readings are possible within certain frames of reference. We are then confined neither to one-sided emphasis nor to endless proliferation of meaning. As is evident from the rhetorical reading applied to *Madame Bovary*, once a particular framework for reading has been chosen, such a reading is necessarily context-bound.

F O U R

Proust's Palimpsest: Multiple Frames of Reference
in *A la recherche du temps perdu*

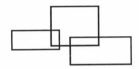

---

*J'aime assez qu'en une oeuvre d'art, on retrouve ainsi transposé, à l'échelle
des personnages le sujet même de cette oeuvre. Rien ne l'éclaire mieux et
n'établit plus sûrement toutes les proportions de l'ensemble.*—G I D E, *Journal*

A striking similarity between *Madame Bovary* and *A la recherche
du temps perdu* is the central importance given to the question
of reading. Both novels include detailed descriptions of how
their central characters read and respond to works of art.
While the focus in *Madame Bovary* is on negative versions of
reading that warn us, through irony, about the dangers of misreading, Proust's novel abounds in models of reading designed to show how the fictions of art and literature set in motion a process of reading that is creative, not destructive.
Though Proust's narrator also gives a few examples of how not
to read, the accent is on the positive as we follow the protagonist's progress from simplistic readings to careful interpretive
readings and rereadings that eventually lead to self-exploration and artistic creation.[1] What is important, in the reading of

---

1. In a deconstructive reading of *A la recherche*, Paul de Man comes to another
conclusion. Though he identifies reading, as I do, as the central frame of reference in Proust's text, he denies it any constructive function in the reading
process, as is obvious from the following quotation: "Everything in this novel

both novels, is to discover how exemplary readings influence our own reading and response to the novel. Since Proust's reader covers many pages and is taken through more than one frame of reference before realizing the central importance given to reading, my emphasis will be on a sequential reading of the novel in order to show how various systems of reference are introduced and how they jointly structure our reading.[2]

On first reading the opening pages of *A la recherche*, the reader, confronted with private talk about bedtime habits some time in the past, rendered in first-person narration, may well expect that this will be a novel of personal history, an autobiographical narrative told in the form of a quest, as promised by the title. But as he reads on, he soon realizes that he cannot complacently settle down in this frame of reference. For one thing, there is a hectic juggling of time, place, and perspective that has a definite disorienting effect, since the reader is not in any one place long enough to find his bearings. For instance, the hero is middle-aged in one paragraph and a child in the next, while point of view abruptly changes from one sentence to another, sliding from the young hero's naive perspective to the narrator's voice of experience.

We are quite aware of such abrupt juxtapositions right from the start of *Combray*. Though the first sentence, "Longtemps, je me suis couché de bonne heure" ("For a long time I used to go to bed early"), initiates the voyage into the past, there is nothing precise about it, since we are given no further details

---

signifies something other than what it represents, be it love, consciousness, politics, art, sodomy, or gastronomy: it is always something else that is intended. It can be shown that the most adequate term to designate this 'something else' is Reading. But one must at the same time 'understand' that this word bars access, once and forever, to a meaning that yet can never cease to call out for its understanding" (*Allegories of Reading* [New Haven: Yale University Press, 1979], p. 77). De Man paradoxically concludes that *A la recherche* is an allegory of reading that narrates the impossibility of reading (p. 77).

2. An abridged version of this chapter has appeared in *Poetics Today* (1983): 89–97 under the title "Reference and the Reader."

as to when and where this happened—the kind of precision we would expect to find in an autobiographical account designed to recapture the past. Only by inference, two paragraphs later, do we see that this early-to-bed period is not part of childhood, that we have landed somewhere in a more recent past: "En dormant j'avais rejoint sans effort un âge à jamais révolu de ma vie primitive, retrouvé telle de mes terreurs enfantines comme celle que mon grand-oncle me tirât par mes boucles."[3] ("While sleeping I had drifted back to an earlier stage in my life, now for ever outgrown, and had come under the thrall of one of my childish terrors, such as that old terror of my great-uncle's pulling my curls"). We now must deal with a double-layered past, since this early-bedtime period is revealed as a springboard to a more distant past.[4] What follows is a juggling of time frames as different periods and places of the hero's past are briefly recalled (1:4–9), while we are reminded more than once that it is affective, not voluntary, memory that initiates the search. This emphasis on affective memory is the first key to an understanding of the kind of journey that leads to the past. It also calls attention to an important aspect of Proustian narrative: in addition to *what* is dis-

---

3. Marcel Proust, *A la recherche du temps perdu*, 3 vols., Pléiade edition (Paris: Gallimard, 1954), 1:4. The English translation that follows is from *Remembrance of Things Past*, trans. C. K. Scott Moncrieff and Terence Kilmartin, 3 vols. (New York: Random House, 1981), 1:4. Hereafter, volume and page references to both these sources are given sequentially within parentheses. Parenthetical references to only one source are to the French edition.

4. The remembering self that bridges the gap between past and present is somewhere around middle age, subject to insomnia and irregular sleeping habits, which turn out to be a blessing in disguise, since they initiate a series of memory trips into the past. It is this "intermediary self" that we encounter in the opening pages of the novel. We lose sight of it as we enter the hero's childhood period in Combray (1:9–43) but are suddenly reminded of it near the end of the first part of *Combray* (1:43), and once more at the end of the second part (1:186). In his study *Les Voix narratives dans "La Recherche du temps perdu"* (Geneva: Librairie Droz, 1965), Marcel Muller calls this voice the *Sujet intermédiaire*, defined as "the *I* which is an indispensable relay enabling the Narrator to remember the Hero" (p. 8, my translation).

covered or rediscovered, considerable time is spent analyzing *how* this is done. At the same time, we are given important pieces of time "lost" already "recovered"—which reveals, at this early stage of our reading, that the intermediary, remembering self is not merely an important agent in the search but that it has been cast as the narrator's muse.[5]

Besides the temporal sliding and the repeated focus on the remembering self, the insistent foregrounding of the narrator's voice of experience—already revealing what the hero has yet to discover—takes us beyond the framework of the autobiographical quest. This voice of experience is the reader's companion throughout the novel. By anticipating knowledge the hero only gradually acquires in the one-directional course of events, the narrator shifts emphasis from quest to disclosure, from the personal to a more global perspective. This dialogic interplay of two contrasting perspectives sets up a "twisted tale" in which personal narrative repeatedly gives way to the study of perception, memory, cognition, and the discovery of truths.[6] This constant movement beyond storytelling calls attention to the fact that the primary focus of *A la recherche* is not the hero's personal history but the narrator's eagerness to intellectualize—to comment, explain, and draw conclusions.

The narrator's intrusions into the hero's world range from subtle intimations to emphatic disclosures. For instance, while

5. The next memorable example will be the description of the hero's first experience of involuntary memory, the madeleine episode at the end of the first part of *Combray* (1:44–48), followed, intermittently, by other examples throughout *A la recherche*, with a final crescendo of several such experiences at the end of the novel, in *Le Temps retrouvé*.

6. Nelson Goodman, in examining different kinds of "twisted tales," shows how they take the reader beyond the framework of the story: "Twisted Tales; or, Story, Study, and Symphony," *Critical Inquiry* 7 (1980): 103–20. See also Dorrit Cohn's discussion of distancing techniques between narrating and experiencing self in Proust's narrative (*Transparent Minds*, pp. 147–51). She groups Proust's novel under "dissonant narration" and concludes that the method used for rendering the hero's consciousness is essentially one of elucidation and interpretation (p. 151).

describing his first experience of involuntary memory, he stays close to the hero's perspective, taking us step by step through his initial bafflement, the questions he asks himself while trying to solve the mystery, and the partial answers he discovers (1:44–48). Though the narrator interpolates explanatory remarks about the lasting impact of sensory impressions while admitting that he now knows more than he did then, he does not give away the secret: "quoique je ne susse pas encore et dusse remettre à bien plus tard de découvrir pourquoi ce souvenir me rendait si heureux" ("although I did not yet know and must long postpone the discovery of why this memory made me so happy") (1:47; translation, 1:51). By calling attention to what remains unsaid, he encourages us to participate in an ongoing process of questions and gradually evolving answers. Though we must wait until the last volume to find the answer, we are thus initiated, in the early stages of reading, into one of the major puzzles to be solved in the search for time lost.[7]

The narrator's presence is most noticeable when he interrupts his tale to reveal the lasting significance of an experience he has just described. One of the most memorable passages is the one in which he gives his retrospective view of the Sunday afternoons spent reading in the garden of Combray. Additional emphasis is given to the narrator's perspective through the lyrical apostrophe to Sunday afternoons. Such emotional markers reveal his involvement in what he is relating, which, in turn, shapes the reader's attitude toward what is being told.[8] This passage acquires added significance once we realize

7. Though this first experience of involuntary memory does not occur until middle age, the reader encounters it at the outset of his journey. This passage is one of the most striking examples of emphasis through reordering. The next instance of affective memory to be described in detail occurs in *Un amour de Swann*, while Swann is listening to Vinteuil's "little phrase" at the St.-Euverte gathering (1:345–47). In subsequent volumes, the reader is periodically reminded of this unique kind of experience so central to the quest.

8. Gérard Genette discusses this testimonial or "emotive" function in "Dis-

that the narrator does not content himself with an abstract account but uses figurative language and complicated syntax to translate the perceptual complexity of the experience.[9] The reader is thus given one more example of the past already recaptured—through both memory and verbal transcription:

> Beaux après-midi du dimanche sous le marronnier du jardin de Combray, soigneusement vidés par moi des incidents médiocres de mon existence personnelle que j'y avais remplacés par une vie d'aventures et d'aspirations étranges au sein d'un pays arrosé d'eaux vives, vous m'évoquez encore cette vie quand je pense à vous et vous la contenez en effet pour l'avoir peu à peu contournée et enclose—tandis que je progressais dans ma lecture et que tombait la chaleur du jour—dans le cristal successif, lentement changeant et traversé de feuillages, de vos heures silencieuses, sonores, odorantes et limpides.

> Sweet Sunday afternoons beneath the chestnut–tree in the garden at Combray, carefully purged by me of every commonplace incident of my personal existence, which I had replaced with a life of strange adventures and aspirations in a land watered with living streams, you still recall that life to me when I think of you, and you embody it in effect by virtue of having gradually encircled and enclosed it— while I went on with my reading and the heat of the day declined—in the crystalline succession, slowly changing and dappled with foliage, of your silent, sonorous, fragrant, limpid hours. (1:88; translation, 1:94–95)

---

cours du récit," p. 262. Proust's narrator actually supplies the reader with an indirect reading model of such emotionally charged passages when he describes the hero's response to Bergotte's novels, pointing out that passages with invocations and apostrophe came across as the most important (1:95).

9. For a detailed analysis of the role of metaphor in this passage, see Inge Crosman, "Metaphoric Function in *A la recherche du temps perdu*," *Romanic Review* 67 (1976): 295–99.

Such dramatic intrusions into the narrative account of the hero's experience have an important function in the reading process. They catch the reader's attention, invite him to ask questions, and involve him more actively in the novel's constant movement beyond narrative.

Our impression that Proust's narrator takes us beyond the borders of a personal narrative is reinforced through the repeated use of iterative narration. Instead of relating his experiences one by one, the narrator groups them in a synthesizing narration in which emphasis is on the kind of experience described rather than on any single occurrence. As Gérard Genette has pointed out, a heightened process of assimilation and abstraction underlies this kind of narrative procedure and reveals the narrator's strong sense of analogy between experiences.[10] As we make our way through *A la recherche*, we gradually realize that this tendency to draw analogies is central to the narrator's vision and technique and that it plays a major role in our understanding of Proust's novel. It also shapes our reading, since we are repeatedly encouraged to make connections between similar experiences described in the novel.

The first instance of iterative narration directly follows the opening sentence of the novel. It stands out at the head of the second sentence, "Parfois, à peine ma bougie éteinte" ("Sometimes, when I had put out my candle"), and sets up the synthesizing narrative framework for the entire "overture" (1:4–9).[11] The iterative reappears in the opening sentence of the first account of childhood—the Combray period: "A Combray, tous les jours dès la fin de l'après-midi, longtemps avant le moment où il faudrait me mettre au lit" ("At Combray, as

10. The nature and importance of this kind of narrative is discussed by Gérard Genette in "Discours du récit," pp. 145–82. The indices of this synthesizing type of discourse range from specific (*tous les samedis*) to less definite markers (*parfois, quelquefois, souvent, certains jours*).

11. There are one or several iterative markers in just about every paragraph of these opening pages. The exceptions are paragraphs 2 and 5–7.

every afternoon ended, long before the time when I should have to go to bed") (1:9; translation, 1:9). From now on, what characterizes the novel is the alternating rhythm from the iterative mode of narration to what Genette has called "singulative" narration, the single account of something that happened only once.[12]

In setting up his many-layered discourse, Proust's narrator introduces another narrative procedure, which, like the iterative, focuses attention on the kind of experience he is describing. Since we encounter this narrative mode, as we do the iterative, right at the start of the novel, their joint presence has a definite effect. It becomes quite clear that the narrator is taking us beyond the incidental when he conjures up two dramatic scenes in succession—first, a detailed description of a lonely traveler catching a night train (at the end of the first paragraph), and then (in the second paragraph) a whole *mise en scène* involving a helpless, sick person in a strange hotel room in the middle of the night. In both instances, a particular state of being—the uneasiness caused by a new situation—is vividly evoked. In these passages, there is a perceptible shift in focus from personal narrative to a frame of reference with more general implications. What is implied is a similar kind of experience in the world, a certain knowledge and sensibility shared by all alike—including hero, narrator, narratee, and reader.[13] Besides these general implications, the two scenes

12. See Genette, "Discours du récit," p. 146. Scenes that obviously stand out as "singulative" in *Combray* are Swann's visit, the night the mother spends in the hero's room, the episode with the lady in pink, the scenes with Legrandin, the hero as voyeur at Montjouvain, the duchesse de Guermantes at the church wedding, and the Martinville episode. Aside from these, the rest of *Combray*, as Genette has pointed out, "narrates, in the French imperfect tense for repeated action, not what *happened* but what *used to happen* at Combray, regularly, ritually, every day, or every Sunday, or every Saturday, etc." (*Narrative Discourse*, pp. 117–18).

13. The various signs that point to the kind of narratee projected or implied in narrative discourse are discussed by Gerald Prince in "Introduction à l'étude

contribute in setting up the protagonist's special kind of world. As we read on, we soon realize that the unsettling experience of travel and the unknown is obviously an obsession with both hero and narrator.[14] But this we learn only gradually. At first reading, the sudden shift in focus from the hero's personal preoccupations inside his room to the plight of the afflicted in some unknown place is quite disconcerting, since it occurs without any transitional remarks. For instance, the imaginary scene with the night traveler is interpolated into midsentence and takes over the rest of the paragraph—while the reader is left wondering where all this comes from and why it is given. The only link is a momentary sensory impression (a train's whistle) that triggers the imagination:

> Je me demandais quelle heure il pouvait être; j'entendais le sifflement des trains qui, plus ou moins éloigné, comme le chant d'un oiseau dans une forêt, relevant les distances, me décrivait l'étendue de la campagne déserte où le voyageur se hâte vers la station prochaine; et le petit chemin qu'il suit va être gravé dans son souvenir par l'excitation qu'il doit à des lieux nouveaux, à des actes inaccoutumés, à la causerie récente et aux adieux sous la lampe étrangère

du narrataire," pp. 178–96. Gérard Genette refines some of Prince's categories in *Nouveau discours du récit*, pp. 90–93.

14. The first such instance occurs in the "overture," where among the various descriptions of rooms from the past, one stands out: a hotel room in which the young hero suffers, since he is unaccustomed to everything in it (1:8). Another example is the description of the hero's feeling of disorientation caused by the magic lantern, which totally changes the atmosphere in his otherwise familiar room: "Maintenant je ne la reconnaissais plus et j'y étais inquiet, comme dans une chambre d'hôtel ou de 'chalet' où je fusse arrivé pour la première fois en descendant de chemin de fer" ("Now I no longer recognized it, and felt uneasy in it, as in a room in some hotel or chalet, in a place where I had just arrived by train for the first time") (1:9; translation, 1:10). It is remarkable how tightly knit an auto-referential network the narrator sets up, since the explanatory comparison harks back to both imaginary tableaux, that of the traveler and the uneasy hotel guest.

qui le suivent encore dans le silence de la nuit, à la douceur prochaine du retour.

I would ask myself what time it could be; I could hear the
whistling of trains, which, now nearer and now farther
off, punctuating the distance like the note of a bird in a
forest, showed me in perspective the deserted countryside through which a traveller is hurrying towards the
nearby station; and the path he is taking will be engraved
in his memory by the excitement induced by strange sur-
roundings, by unaccustomed activities, by the conversation he has had and the farewells exchanged beneath an
unfamiliar lamp, still echoing in his ears amid the silence
of the night, by the imminent joy of going home. (1:3–4;
translation, 1:3)

Another indication that we are reading within an expanded
frame of reference that takes us beyond personal narration are
inconsistencies in perspective. One of the earliest examples of
improbable narrative focus is the verbatim transcription of the
conversation between Françoise and Tante Léonie, followed
by a brief indication of the hero's whereabouts at that time:
"Pendant que ma tante devisait ainsi avec Françoise, j'accom-
pagnais mes parents à la messe" ("While my aunt was gossip-
ing on in this way with Françoise I accompanied my parents
to mass") (1:59; translation, 1:63). How then, while out of earshot, could he have heard those conversations? Since, given
the conventions of verisimilitude, first-person narration sets
up a restricted field of vision based on the limited knowledge
of the self, such extended vision is registered by the reader as
excess information, as an infraction of the narrative code that
is in force—in short, as an abrupt change in perspective.[15]

15. For distinctions among the different kinds of narrative perspective—ranging from restricted, "focalized" (internal and external focalization) to nonre-
stricted, "unfocalized" narration—see Gérard Genette, "Discours du récit,"
pp. 206–10, and Nouveau discours du récit, pp. 49–50.

Such infractions are found throughout the novel. The most glaring example is, of course, *Un Amour de Swann*. It simply is not possible for anyone to know another person's life to the extent described here, including Swann's most intimate thoughts. The explanation given at the end of *Combray* of how the narrator remembered what he had been told about Swann's love, "dans les détails plus facile à obtenir quelquefois pour la vie de personnes mortes il y a des siècles que pour celle de nos meilleurs amis" ("with a precision of detail which it is often easier to obtain for the lives of people who have been dead for centuries than for those of our own most intimate friends") (1:186; translation, 1:203), is at best a *surjustification*, which, through its conspicuousness, reveals the narrator's need to rationalize. If examined strictly from the standpoint of narrative logic, such invasions of other people's private views are dissonant within autobiographical narration.[16] In conjunction with other narrative practices, abrupt changes from one center of perception to another point to the need to go beyond an autobiographical reading of *A la recherche*, to heed other voices and to become aware of the multiple discourses that shape this novel.

That the narrator speaks in more than one voice is especially noticeable when the reader finds himself straddling discourses

16. In his *Nouveau discours du récit*, Genette introduces the term *préfocalisation* (p. 52) to describe the restricted point of view in first-person narration, a restriction that can only be avoided through transgression. In "Discours du récit" he uses the word *polymodalité* (p. 224) to characterize Proust's narrative, which uses three different and incompatible kinds of focalization, sliding from the hero's to the narrator's consciousness and inhabiting here and there the mind of various characters. He rightly concluded that "this triple narrative position is not at all comparable to the simple omniscience of the classical novel, for it not only defies . . . the conditions of the realistic illusion: it also transgresses a 'law of the spirit' requiring that one cannot be inside and outside at the same time" (*Narrative Discourse*, p. 210). The transgression of first-person narration in Proust's novel through inclusion of a more authoritative, less restricted vision is discussed by Lubomir Doležel in "Truth and Authenticity in Narrative," *Poetics Today* 1 (1980): 20.

while the narrator stops telling his story to generalize or philosophize. This sliding into ideological discourse is a narrative constant in Proust's novel. Its repeated occurrence—introducing a pause into the narrative—marks the rhythm of the novel and can escape no reader.[17] This emphasis on the ideological definitely takes the reader beyond the autobiographical framework. He is quite aware of this frame breaking right from the start of *Combray*, when, in the midst of intimate talk about the hero's sleeping habits, the narrator suddenly introduces explanations about sleep in general. While these generalizing remarks about the disorienting effect of irregular sleep shed light on the hero's predicament by providing a frame of reference for understanding his particular situation, they also implicate the reader through inclusive pronouns and universal claims:

> Un homme qui dort tient en cercle autour de lui le fil des heures, l'ordre des années et des mondes. Il les consulte d'instinct en s'éveillant et y lit en une seconde le point de la terre qu'il occupe, le temps qui s'est écoulé jusqu'à son réveil; mais leurs rangs peuvent se mêler, se rompre.

> When a man is asleep, he has in a circle round him the chain of the hours, the sequence of the years, the order of the heavenly host. Instinctively, when he awakes, he looks to these, and in an instant reads off his own position on the earth's surface and the time that has elapsed during his slumbers; but this ordered procession is apt to grow confused, and to break its ranks. (1:5; translation, 1:5)

What follows this general observation on sleep is the description of various situations that lead to temporal and spatial dis-

---

17. Gérard Genette has pointed out that this ideological voice is one of the narrator's principal functions. He concludes that Proust's novel is perhaps no longer just a novel, because of "this invasion of the story by the commentary, of the novel by the essay, of the narrative by its own discourse" (*Narrative Discourse*, p. 259).

orientation. The narrative then switches back to the hero, linking the general discovery about sleep to his personal situation, which the reader is now better able to understand. As in the previous dramatic scenes about the traveler and the hotel guest, the description of the anonymous sleeper initiates the reader into a *kind* of experience, a particular way of being in and viewing the world. Since, through generalizing discourse, the reader is periodically implicated in the world that gradually emerges, he is led into a more active reading, which enables him to draw analogies between what is presented as general knowledge and the hero's experience.[18] He may also transfer insights gained through reading to his own life, which sets in motion a process of identification between reader and text.[19]

Equally striking, a few pages later and still in the beginning stages of our reading, is the intrusion of a generalizing maxim in the midst of a narrative passage introducing Swann, who, having just arrived to join the hero's family for dinner, is left standing at the door while we are told how "our social personality is created by the thoughts of others." This is one of the novel's key passages and the first in preparing us for the multiple perspectives from which all characters will be viewed. This early insight given us in connection with Swann will resonate in our memory, since the same "truth" about the difficulty of knowing others will be brought home repeatedly, particularly in the narrator's analysis of the elusive personalities

18. See Harald Weinrich's discussion of how reader response is affected by a switch from narrative to non-narrative discourse, with its concomitant changes in the verbal system and personal pronouns, in addition to the sudden presence of "imputative language" such as performatives and other kinds of expressions constituting an act ("Les Temps et les personnes," *Poétique* no. 39 [1979]: 338–52). For a detailed discussion of the role of verbs and pronouns in shaping discourse, see E. Benveniste's *Problèmes de linguistique générale*, chapters 18–20.

19. This "dialogic" interplay in an active response to reading fiction is discussed by Wolfgang Iser in *The Act of Reading*, pp. 129–34.

of Gilberte and Albertine, and the changing image of Mme. de Guermantes. Like the previous passage on sleep, the present one makes claims that reach beyond the story world:

Mais même au point de vue des plus insignifiantes choses de la vie, nous ne sommes pas un tout matériellement constitué, identique pour tout le monde et dont chacun n'a qu'à aller prendre connaissance comme d'un cahier des charges ou d'un testament; notre personnalité sociale est une création de la pensée des autres. Même l'acte si simple que nous appelons "voir une personne que nous connaissons" est en partie un acte intellectuel. Nous remplissons l'apparence physique de l'être que nous voyons de toutes les notions que nous avons sur lui, et dans l'aspect total que nous nous représentons, ces notions ont certainement la plus grande part. Elles finissent par gonfler si parfaitement les joues, par suivre en une adhérence si exacte la ligne du nez, elles se mêlent si bien de nuancer la sonorité de la voix comme si celle-ci n'était qu'une transparente enveloppe, que chaque fois que nous voyons ce visage et que nous entendons cette voix, ce sont ces notions que nous retrouvons, que nous écoutons.

But then, even in the most insignificant details of our daily life, none of us can be said to constitute a material whole, which is identical for everyone, and need only be turned up like a page in an account-book or the record of a will; our social personality is a creation of the thoughts of other people. Even the simple act which we describe as "seeing someone we know" is to some extent an intellectual process. We pack the physical outline of the person we see with all the notions we have already formed about him, and in the total picture of him which we compose in our minds those notions have certainly the principal place. In the end they come to fill out so completely the curve of his cheeks, to follow so exactly the line of his nose, they blend so harmoniously in the sound of his voice as if it were no more than a transparent envelope, that each time we see the face or hear the voice it is these notions which we recognise and to which we listen. (1:19; translation, 1:20)

The sudden interpolation of this interpretive voice into the midst of the story, and the considerable extent to which it goes on—carefully analyzing a subtle insight first intended to elucidate a point in the story (why people have such different impressions of Swann), and then proclaiming it, with the voice of authority, as a general truth—stands out in the text and commands attention. Our increasing awareness of the alternating rhythm between the narrative voice that tells the story and another that interprets and generalizes has a definite effect in shaping our response to the novel. We no longer take it as simply a fiction intended to divert us, but as a book designed to teach us.

Even more striking than this repeated interpolation of general commentary into the framework of a personal story is the fact that an entire volume is devoted to Swann. This unexpected focus on a secondary character in a first-person novel, along with a change from first-person to what is predominantly third-person narration, is the novel's biggest interpretive puzzle. The reader's first impression of *Un amour de Swann* is one of utter *dépaysement*. From the privacy of the hero's bedroom and the intimacy of first-person narration—both well established by the end of *Combray*—the reader is thrown into a beginning in medias res with an entirely new setting: another era, another social milieu, different characters. The absence of any transition between *Combray* and *Swann* certainly commands attention and raises a number of questions.

Though we begin to get our bearings when five paragraphs later Swann is mentioned within the setting of a love intrigue, as promised by the title, it soon becomes clear that the narrator takes us beyond the simple telling of a story. We infer, and are repeatedly encouraged to infer, that Swann's story stands for more than itself. Several aspects of Proustian narrative converge to make this point; for instance, while describing Swann's vanity, the narrator adds a judgmental, parenthetical remark about wasting artistic talent in social pursuits, which is an important sign of another quest—the quest for knowledge and a true vocation, which will turn out to be of central importance in the hero's search:

> Car le désir ou l'amour lui rendait alors un sentiment de vanité dont il était maintenant exempt dans l'habitude de la vie (bien que ce fût lui sans doute qui autrefois l'avait dirigé vers cette carrière mondaine où il avait gaspillé dans les plaisirs frivoles les dons de son esprit et fait servir son érudition en matière d'art à conseiller les dames de la société dans leurs achats de tableaux et pour l'ameublement de leurs hôtels), et qui lui faisait désirer de briller, aux yeux d'une inconnue dont il s'était épris, d'une élégance que le nom de Swann à lui tout seul n'impliquait pas.

> For at such times desire, or love, would revive in him a feeling of vanity from which he was now quite free in his everyday life (although it was doubtless this feeling which had originally prompted him towards the career as a man of fashion in which he had squandered his intellectual gifts on frivolous amusements and made use of his erudition in matters of art only to advise society ladies what pictures to buy and how to decorate their houses), which made him eager to shine, in the eyes of any fair unknown whom he had fallen for, with an elegance which the name Swann did not in itself imply. (1:191; translation, 1:208–209)

It is significant that in subsequent passages Swann is repeatedly judged for misusing his artistic and intellectual talents.[20]

20. For instance: "pour lui dont les yeux, quoique délicats amateurs de pein-

That more than Swann's life is at stake becomes even more obvious a few lines later when the voice of opinion leaves Swann altogether in order to focus on human behavior in general:

De même que ce n'est pas à un autre homme intelligent qu'un homme intelligent aura peur de paraître bête, ce n'est pas par un grand seigneur, c'est par un rustre qu'un homme élégant craindra de voir son élégance méconnue. Les trois quarts des frais d'esprit et des mensonges de vanité qui ont été prodigués depuis que le monde existe par des gens qu'ils ne faisaient que diminuer, l'ont été pour des inférieurs.

Just as it is not by other men of intelligence that an intelligent man is afraid of being thought a fool, so it is not by a nobleman but by an oaf that a man of fashion is afraid of finding his social value underrated. Three-quarters of the mental ingenuity and the mendacious boasting squandered ever since the world began by people who are only cheapened thereby, have been aimed at inferiors. (1:191; translation, 1:209)

This long analogy, introduced to explain why Swann, at ease with a duchess, trembles in front of a chambermaid, re-introduces the reader to a voice already familiar to him—the voice given to general observations about the ways of the world. As in *Combray*, the narrator's interruption of the forward movement of the story to insert general observations, and the contrasts in discourse created through sudden changes in tense,

---

ture, dont l'esprit, quoique fin observateur de moeurs, portaient à jamais la trace indélébile de la sécheresse de sa vie" ("whose eyes, although delicate interpreters of painting, whose mind, although an acute observer of manners, must bear for ever the indelible imprint of the barrenness of his life") (1:237; translation, 1:259) and "ayant laissé s'affaiblir les croyances intellectuelles de sa jeunesse" ("having allowed the intellectual beliefs of his youth to languish") (1:247; translation, 1:269). Moreover, on pp. 248 and 273–74 the reader is explicitly told about Swann's misplaced passion for truth.

pronouns, and focus, command attention. That the field of vision extends beyond Swann's life becomes even more evident when the narrator repeatedly interpolates generalizing passages ranging from brief analogies that shed light on Swann's particular situation to long digressions during which the reader loses sight of him.[21]

More striking than the rediscovery of the voice of wisdom is the sudden reappearance (in the ninth paragraph) of the first-person pronoun (1:193).[22] However brief this intrusion, it reminds us of the principal frame of narration. This impression is reinforced when the narrator refers to himself by situating Swann's love affair in reference to his own life:

> Je me suis souvent fait raconter bien des années plus tard, quand je commençai à m'intéresser à son caractère à cause des ressemblances qu'en de tout autres parties il offrait avec le mien, que quand il écrivait à mon grand-père (qui ne l'était pas encore, car c'est vers l'époque de ma naissance que commença la grande liaison de Swann, et elle interrompit longtemps ces pratiques), celui-ci, en reconnaissant sur l'enveloppe l'écriture de son ami, s'écriait: "Voilà Swann qui va demander quelque chose: à la garde!"

> I used often to be told, many years later, when I began to take an interest in his character because of the similarities which, in wholly different respects, if offered to my own, how, when he used to write to my grandfather (who had not yet become my grandfather, for it was about the time of my birth that Swann's great love affair began, and it made a long interruption in his amatory practices), the lat-

---

21. The most noticeable and memorable are long deliberations on the nature of love, providing the reader with a whole philosophy of love that serves as an interpretive background against which he reads Swann's love affair, and later, the hero's.

22. The first person reappears on pp. 295, 297, 309–12, 358, 378, 381.

ter, recognising his friend's handwriting on the envelope,
would exclaim: "Here's Swann asking for something. On
guard!" (1:193–94; translation, 1:211)

Besides momentarily returning us to the frame of reference of
first-person narration, the overt analogy between Swann's
character and the narrator's, explicitly given as a reason for his
interest in Swann, provides us with an important key for reading this volume. By stressing kinships and contrasts between
them, the narrator invites a comparative reading during which
we begin to suspect that Swann is no longer a character in his
own right, but in many ways the hero-narrator's alter ego.[23]
Once we realize that Swann's status changes from person to
"figure," we can no longer read literally and are initiated into
what will turn out to be the principal mode for reading the
novel, that is, analogically. Through analogies and contrasts
we become involved in a tightly knit dialogic structure that
takes us from the primary level of meaning where incidental
episodes exist in their own right to an interpretive reading that
discloses their significance and expands the frame of reference.[24]

23. More than one narrative technique points to these broader implications. In
addition to general observations and critical comments, the narrator makes
remarks that reveal his emotional involvement in Swann's life. This is particularly evident when he hypothesizes and empathizes, interjecting emotional
outcries that reveal his vicarious participation; for example, "Ah! avec quelle
joie . . . il eût grimpé les étages noirs" ("Ah, with what joy . . . would he have
raced up the dark . . . flights") (1:324; translation, 1:353) or "Ah! comme il eût
aimé la connaître" ("Ah, how he would have loved to know her") (1:318;
translation, 1:347). It is noteworthy that the first parallel between Swann and
the protagonist is set up in *Combray* when the narrator describes the hero's
anguish while waiting for his mother. Swann, the reader is told, would have
understood such anguish caused by the prolonged absence of a loved one
(1:30).
24. Swann is not the only character who stands for more than himself. In *La
Prisonnière*, Albertine is described as "une grande déesse du Temps" ("a
mighty goddess of Time") (3:387; translation, 3:393), and Mlle. de Saint-Loup
turns out to be a "symbol of time" in *Le Temps retrouvé* (3:1029–32). I have
discussed elsewhere how the entire description of the Matinée Guermantes

This kind of referential expansion is most apparent when the narrator describes Swann's experience of listening to the Vinteuil Sonata. Swann first serves as a model reader whose progressive insight into Vinteuil's music is stressed when the narrator highlights the difference between first and subsequent listenings while emphasizing the role of memory in helping him grasp the music's overall design (1:208–10). By dwelling on the emotional and intellectual pleasures of the listening experience, and by insisting on its transcendent nature, the narrator calls attention to the privileged nature of this kind of experience.[25] That such an experience ought to be explored to the fullest is the lesson to be inferred by the reader from the critical distance from which Swann is viewed in the following pages (1:210–11, 218). Dissonant narration is set up through the dialogic opposition of two perspectives: on the one hand, the narrator's view of what this experience could and should be for Swann; on the other, Swann's wrong choice. He ends up as the narrator's foil when he trivializes art by giving it a personalized, banal reading, associating the music with his love for Odette. Instead of looking for its intrinsic value, Swann now sees Vinteuil's "little phrase" as "the national hymn of their love" (1:218). Swann's choice is dramatically undermined through the narrator's presentational process. By repeatedly describing the musical phrase in terms of an irresist-

---

takes on symbolic implications when the narrator repeatedly focuses on the aged appearance of everyone present (Inge Crosman, *Metaphoric Narration: The Structure and Function of Metaphors in "A la recherche du temps perdu"* [Chapel Hill: University of North Carolina Press, 1978], pp. 143–60).

25. We are told that the music takes Swann "vers un bonheur noble," "des perspectives inconnues" ("towards a state of happiness that was noble," "towards new vistas") (1:210; translation, 1:228–29) and reveals to him "la présence d'une de ces réalités invisibles auxquelles il avait cessé de croire" ("the presence of one of those invisible realities in which he had ceased to believe") (1:211; translation, 1:230). From these and similar passages it is obvious that Swann, in more ways than one, is the protagonist's spiritual father. The reader is explicitly told this in *Le Temps retrouvé* (3:915) when the narrator gives Swann credit for providing him with material for a book.

ible woman (1:209–10, 211–12, 264), he sets it up as Odette's rival: "Il avait éprouvé pour elle *comme un amour inconnu*" ("He had been filled with love for it, *as with a new and strange desire*") (1:210; my italics; 1:228, my italics). Yet Swann opts for Odette.

The narrator's dissonant view becomes more obvious when he takes over and gives his own version of musical listening (1:218, 264), providing the reader with a verbal transcription of the music's sound and movement, thus showing him, through a contrastive reading, how to capture the essence of the "little phrase," how to go beyond Swann's sterile reading, which never gets off the ground.

That more than Swann's musical listening is at stake is obvious when the narrator introduces general insights about music while describing Swann's experience. Music is revealed as a unique mode of communication and a way of conquering death, since it is able to translate and preserve feelings and insights.[26] In this context, the narrator speaks in a more inclusive, general voice and in a lyrical tone, both a dramatic testimonial to the importance he attaches to these observations. For instance, the striking image of unexplored worlds and a switch in pronoun to the first-person plural set the message in relief in the following passage about the range of emotions that music can express:

Il savait que . . . le champ ouvert au musicien n'est pas un clavier mesquin de sept notes, mais un clavier incommensurable, encore presque tout entier inconnu, où seulement ça et là, séparées par d'épaisses ténèbres inexplorées, quelques-unes des millions de touches de tendresse, de passion, de courage, de sérénité, qui le composent, chacune aussi différente des autres qu'un univers d'un autre univers, ont été découvertes par quelques

26. See, for example, 1:349, where the reader is told how the "little phrase" is able to capture and recreate "les charmes d'une tristesse intime" ("the charms of an intimate sadness") (translation, 1:379).

grands artistes qui nous rendent le service, en éveillant en nous le correspondant du thème qu'ils ont trouvé, de nous montrer quelle richesse, quelle variété, cache à notre insu cette grande nuit impénétrée et décourageante de notre âme que nous prenons pour du vide et pour du néant.

He knew that . . . the field open to the musician is not a miserable stave of seven notes, but an immeasurable keyboard (still almost entirely unknown) on which, here and there only, separated by the thick darkness of its unexplored tracts, some few among the millions of keys of tenderness, of passion, of courage, of serenity, which compose it, each one differing from all the rest as one universe differs from another, have been discovered by a few great artists who do us the service, when they awaken in us the emotion corresponding to the theme they have discovered, of showing us what richness, what variety lies hidden, unknown to us, in that vast, unfathomed and forbidding night of our soul which we take to be an impenetrable void. (1:349–50; translation, 1:380)

Here and elsewhere—through the metaphor of the quest and conquest of unexplored worlds—the narrator brings home the fact that the quest that really matters is the search within.[27] By not realizing this, Swann misdirects his whole life. The reader now understands, in retrospect, why the narrator, in an earlier passage describing Swann's deficient musical listening, leveled a sweeping criticism at the course his life was taking: "Depuis si longtemps il avait renoncé à appliquer sa vie à un but idéal et la bornait à la poursuite de satisfactions quotidiennes" ("He had so long ceased to direct his life towards any ideal goal, confining himself to the pursuit of ephemeral satisfac-

27. Artists are described as "explorers of the invisible," having access to a "divine world" (1:351). Similar analogies stressing the creation of a new world through art reappear throughout *A la recherche*.

tions"), followed a few lines later by "Aussi avait-il pris l'habitude de se réfugier dans des pensées sans importance qui lui
permettaient de laisser de côté le fond des choses"[28] ("Thus he
had grown into the habit of taking refuge in trivial considerations, which enabled him to disregard matters of fundamental
importance") (1:210; translation, 1:229).

The corrective description of Swann's listening experience,
backed up by interpretive commentary with general implications, provides the reader with the first outline of an aesthetic
reading model, to be developed later through recurring descriptions of music and analogies to other art forms. Vinteuil's
music is mentioned again in the next volume (*A l'ombre des
jeunes filles en fleurs*) within the context of the hero's story,
which is taken up again right after *Un amour de Swann*. When
the narrator describes how the hero listens to Vinteuil's music
at Swann's house, emphasis is once more on the, by now,
well-known "little phrase," and the reader is explicitly reminded that this is "la Sonate de Vinteuil où se trouve la petite
phrase que Swann avait tant aimée" ("the passage in Vinteuil's sonata that contained the little phrase of which Swann
had been so fond") (1:529; translation, 1:570). This reminder
refers the reader to parts of the story already told and invites
a comparative scanning between this and earlier descriptions
of the music.

The most striking difference is the predominance of generalizing remarks in this passage (1:529–34). Instead of focusing
on the listener and his first experience with the music, the narrator anticipates by bringing in the hero's subsequent exposure to the music in order to draw certain conclusions. What
follows is a long deliberation on the role of memory in the per-

28. Swann thus gradually emerges as a failed artist. The presence, in Proust's
novel, of two kinds of artists—real ones and *artistes manqués*—is discussed by
Jean Rousset in *Forme et signification*, pp. 147–49. He is right to emphasize that
"Swann and Charlus are, in *La Recherche*, negative images of the great artists,
Elstir and Vinteuil" (p. 148, my translation).

ception of music, formulated in general terms, with occasional applications to the hero's experience. What is obviously important is not the single experience but the insights to be gleaned from it.

Two important facts, both related to memory, emerge from this episode. One of these is the categorical difference between the first and subsequent exposures to a piece of music: while first listenings are overwhelming in their constant flux of new impressions, second listenings, with the help of memory, enable one to notice qualitative differences and structural relationships. The second fact that the narrator dwells on is the role of time: "La mélancolie qui s'attache à la connaissance de tels ouvrages, comme de tout ce qui se réalise dans le temps" ("The melancholy inseparable from one's knowledge of such works, as of everything that takes place in time") (1:530; translation, 1:571). Not only time and memory are linked in this context, but also music and other experiences in life—a point made a few lines later: "Pour n'avoir pu aimer qu'en des temps successifs tout ce que m'apportait cette Sonate, je ne la possédai jamais tout entière: elle ressemblait à la vie" ("Since I was able to enjoy everything that this sonata had to give me only in a succession of hearings, I never possessed it in its entirety: it was like life itself") (1:530; translation, 1:571). This revelation is qualified in the next sentence by an additional piece of wisdom, prophetic, in its implications, of the direction the protagonist's quest will take and of the novel's development: while life begins, we are told, by giving away the best it has to offer, works of art are always open to new discoveries.

All that has been said about memory, time, and the essential difference between first and second "readings" may, by implication, be applied to our reading of *A la recherche*. Viewed this way, all musical descriptions and commentary provide us with a reading model that is both literal, in that it describes a particular experience of listening, and symbolic or allegorical, in that it has an analogical and didactic function. That musical descriptions function as reading models is obvious once more when Swann's response to the music is juxtaposed with the hero-narrator's transcendent reading. It is quite evident that Swann's version serves as a negative model when the narrator openly criticizes him for associating the music with the setting in which it was heard instead of looking for a deeper meaning (1:533–34). Since the same kind of corrective, higher reading is added to the various naive readings of the novel's hero as well, we begin to see Swann and the hero as participants in an "allegory of reading." Similarly, we begin to see ourselves as involved in a "reading of readings" while the narrator weaves his increasingly complex texture of consonant, dissonant, and transcendent narration, in a discursive movement where transcendent narration gains momentum, establishing itself as the dominant discourse by the time we reach the last volume.

As we go through *Swann* and *A l'ombre des jeunes filles en fleurs*, it becomes increasingly clear that the narrator is setting up multiple frames of reference while moving beyond autobiographical discourse. The novel's central purpose, its narrative and thematic matrix, becomes all the more conspicuous when our attention is repeatedly focused on a variety of artists and their work, including music, painting, and literature. It is evident from the manner in which they are discussed that these art forms are not Swann's or the hero's incidental pastimes. While each work and the particular type of response it elicits are described in great detail, what is even more striking is the insertion of interpretive remarks disclosing the "truths" discovered through art. Through repetition, the various art works' joint role becomes apparent. They exemplify artistic processes, play a role in the hero's intellectual and aesthetic quest, and provide us with timely reading models setting the hermeneutic process in motion.[29] Retrospectively we realize

29. The function, within certain literary works, of other art works intended as *mise en abyme*, through analogy, is discussed by Lucien Dällenbach in "Intertexte et autotexte," *Poétique* 27 (1976): 291–95.

that from *Swann* on, the novel unfolds as a *Bildungsroman*, in particular, a *Künstlerroman*. This, rather than the focus on any one character, is what gives the novel its narrative unity.[30]

In addition to Vinteuil's music, which is the first reading model to set up an expanded frame of reference that initiates us into a "higher" reading, the detailed treatment of Elstir's paintings stands out.[31] The most striking example is the hero's first encounter with his art in *A l'ombre* (1:834–40). The narrator's metaphorical description of the optical illusions in one of Elstir's paintings is a verbal tour de force that catches our attention, as does his repeated emphasis on the role of perspective in creating such mirages. From interpolated commentary

30. How narrative unity is achieved through significant repetition is discussed by Maurizio Ferraris and Daniela de Agostini in "Proust, Deleuze et la répétition: Notes sur les niveaux narratifs d'*A la recherche du temps perdu*," *Littérature*, no. 32 (December 1978): 66–85.

31. For the repeated focus on Elstir see, for example, 1:834–40, 847–65, 897–902, 924–25; 2:125–26, 419–22, 500, 523. Retrospectively, the reader also sees the significance of the close account of the young hero's impression of Bergotte's novels over which the narrator lingered in *Combray* (1:93–97). In *A l'ombre* (1:555–57, 561–62, 570), Bergotte's aesthetic practice is upheld while Norpois's mistaken criticism of him is ironically dismissed (1:472–74). Bergotte himself makes a plea for a more "colourful" style when he compares his writing to Vermeer's painting (3:186–88). While the striking metaphorical style and ideological component of Bergotte's novels resonate with *A la recherche*, the long pastiche of the Goncourts' writing stands in sharp contrast to the novel we are reading and is obviously intended as a negative model (*Le Temps retrouvé* 3:709–21).

Other reading models that stand out in *A la recherche* include the description of the hero's reactions to la Berma's performances in *Phèdre*—the first of which is obviously intended as a naive, incomplete reading (1:445–51, 456–58, 480–81), while the hero's second reading is exemplary and is explicitly linked to the lesson learned from Elstir (2:46–52). By the time the reader gets to *La Prisonnière*, the hero has had extensive experience with the various art forms, which is reflected in the comparative readings that are now given; for example, Vinteuil, Wagner, and Balzac are linked in one context (3:158–62), while, in another, Vinteuil, Dostoyevsky, and Vermeer are compared (3:371–87). The long analysis and metaphorical transcription of Vinteuil's Septuor (3:248–61), contrasted here with the earlier Sonata, is perhaps the most striking model for aesthetic reception Proust's reader has yet encountered.

we learn the importance of perspective in re-creating the illusions of first impressions, a technique, we are told, that gives us new ways of looking at the world, a new image "singulière et pourtant vraie, et qui à cause de cela est pour nous doublement saisissante parce qu'elle nous étonne, nous fait sortir de nos habitudes et tout à la fois nous fait rentrer en nous-même en nous rappelant une impression"[32] ("unusual and yet true to nature, and for that reason doubly striking because it surprises us, takes us out of our cocoon of habit, and at the same time brings us back to ourselves by recalling an earlier impression") (1:838; translation, 1:896–97). The importance of new ways of seeing is one of the novel's major revelations. Here it is one of the early clues to the kind of quest the reader is engaged in, and, by inference, the role of *A la recherche* in getting him there.

The artistic insight gained from Elstir's painting is closely tied to the experience of the hero, who, during his first visit to Balbec, decides to make the most of his stay by looking at things and people in a new and open way.[33] While extolling this new vision and "le trouble délicieux de se mêler à une vie inconnue" ("the disturbing thrill of being involved in an unfamiliar way of life") (1:678; translation, 1:729), he feels sorry

32. The implications for the literary work of art can easily be inferred from Proust's play with perspective. The parallel is made obvious when the narrator compares the mirages of Elstir's seascapes to the function of metaphor: "Mais j'y pouvais discerner que le charme de chacune consistait en une sorte de métamorphose des choses représentées, analogue à celle qu'en poésie on nomme métaphore" ("But I was able to discern from these that the charm of each of them lay in a sort of metamorphosis of the objects represented, analogous to what in poetry we call metaphor") (1:835; translation, 1:893). In "Reading a Painting by Elstir," P.W.M. Cogman points out that most of Elstir's paintings are "not best interpreted primarily as a painting; Proust is not trying to describe a picture straightforwardly, but rather to evoke a literary parallel to it, an analogue or *double*" (*French Studies* 30 [1976]: 421).

33. The lesson learned from Elstir is one of vision, as the narrator openly acknowledges: he has taught him how to perceive analogies (1:811), how to find beauty in the simplest things, and how to apply art to life (1:851–52, 869).

for the other hotel guests who, locked into their habitual frame of mind, see nothing. This is not the reader's plight, since as readers we are invited to participate in this exploratory vision through the narrator's metaphorical re-creations. We are thus able to see, for instance, the ocean as a circus and snowy mountains (1:672–73), a hotel clerk as a small potted tree (1:706, 723), and the Balbec dining room as a beehive (1:806) and an aquarium (1:681).[34]

All this confirms that the lesson learned from Elstir's art is one of vision. Since such creative vision can be turned into works of art, as we have seen in the case of Elstir's paintings and the narrator's ability to recapture the fleeting impressions of his past through metaphor, works of art are revealed as "ways of worldmaking"—a significant discovery that the narrator emphatically voices more than once.[35] The implications, for protagonist and reader, of the artists encountered in the quest, are made explicit when the narrator sets up an analogy between Vinteuil, Elstir, and artists in general:

> Le seul véritable voyage, le seul bain de Jouvence, ce ne serait pas d'aller vers de nouveaux paysages, mais d'avoir d'autres yeux, de voir l'univers avec les yeux d'un autre, de cent autres, de voir les cent univers que chacun d'eux voit, que chacun d'eux est; et cela nous le pouvons avec un Elstir, avec un Vinteuil, avec leurs pareils, nous volons vraiment d'étoiles en étoiles.

34. Other striking passages of analogical vision within the Balbec context include another metaphorical description of the sea (1:802–805), the description of the grandmother's room (1:704–705), the portrayal of the beauty of apple trees (1:707), the description of the restaurant at Rivebelle as seen through the eyes of the inebriated protagonist (1:809–14), the "still-life" description of a fish (1:694–95) and fruit (1:698), and the recurring metaphorical depiction of the group of young girls on the Balbec beach (1:788–98, 823–24, 830–32; 855).
35. See, for example, 2:327–28 and 3:159–60, 254–58, 375, 895–1023. To what extent our universe consists of "ways of describing" rather than of a world, or of worlds, is discussed by Nelson Goodman in *Ways of Worldmaking*.

The only true voyage of discovery, the only really rejuve-
nating experience, would be not to visit strange lands but
to possess other eyes, to see the universe through the
eyes of another, of a hundred others, to see the hundred
universes that each of them sees, that each of them is; and
this we can do with an Elstir, with a Vinteuil; with men
like these we do really fly from star to star. (3:258; translation, 3:260)

The network of associations between the hero, Swann, and
the reader is made even more explicit when the protagonist
turned writer sets up his future book as a reading model, both
for himself and, in a transworld gesture, for the reader.[36]
While *writing* the book allows him to illuminate his own experience, *reading* it will serve, we are told, a similarly useful
purpose:[37]

En réalité, chaque lecteur est, quand il lit, le propre lecteur
de soi-même. L'ouvrage de l'écrivain n'est qu'une espèce
d'instrument optique qu'il offre au lecteur afin de lui per-
mettre de discerner ce que, sans ce livre, il n'eût peut-être

36. Like the Proustian narrator, some current theories of reading encourage
readers to extend text interpretation to self-interpretation. See, for example,
Wolfgang Iser, *The Act of Reading*, parts 3 and 4; Paul Ricoeur, "Qu'est-ce
qu'un texte?" pp. 181–200; Norman N. Holland, "Recovering 'The Purloined
Letter': Reading as a Personal Transaction," in *The Reader in the Text: Essays on
Audience and Interpretation*, ed. Susan R. Suleiman and Inge Crosman (Princeton: Princeton University Press, 1980), pp. 350–70; and David Bleich, *Subjective
Criticism* (Baltimore: Johns Hopkins University Press, 1978).
37. It is again significant that the same message is repeated more than once in
Le Temps retrouvé; for example, in 3:890 the reader is told that writers are
mainly translators, since "ce livre essentiel, le seul livre vrai, un grand écrivain
n'a pas, dans le sens courant, à l'inventer, puisqu'il existe déjà en chacun de
nous, mais à le traduire" ("the essential, the only true book, though in the
ordinary sense of the word it does not have to be 'invented' by a great writer—
for it exists already in each of us—has to be translated by him") (translation,
3:926). See also 3:895–96, where the work of a writer is compared to that of a
photographer who develops pictures—those "negatives" within us that
would otherwise remain useless.

pas vu en soi-même. La reconnaissance en soi-même, par le lecteur, de ce que dit le livre, est la preuve de la vérité de celui-ci, et *vice-versa*, au moins dans une certaine mesure, la différence entre les deux textes pouvant être souvent imputée non à l'auteur mais au lecteur.

In reality every reader is, while he is reading, the reader of his own self. The writer's work is merely a kind of optical instrument which he offers to the reader to enable him to discern what, without this book, he would perhaps never have perceived in himself. And the recognition by the reader in his own self of what the book says is the proof of its veracity, the contrary also being true, at least to a certain extent, for the difference between the two texts may sometimes be imputed less to the author than to the reader. (3:911; translation, 3:949)

It is up to the reader to take over where the writer left off, to complete the quest mapped out in the novel by finding the proper coordinates in a process of self-discovery. By claiming that art, including the very book we are reading, does not exist for its own sake but is an instrument for further knowledge, the narrator supplies us with the novel's ultimate referent. We are now able to see the hero's search as an exemplum, and Proust's novel as a reading model. Retrospectively, we realize that this is the ultimate goal of the quest—a quest into which we are gradually initiated, and in which we participate. Though the quest begins with autobiographical discourse, we are taken far beyond the personal. The novel's movement is from the specific to the general: we are repeatedly referred to *kinds* of experiences and are shown with increasing insistence how the general can be discovered in the specific. This movement toward the general is reflected in the narrator's growing tendency to juxtapose similar experiences in the same narrative context.[38] Yet we are returned to the autobiographical at

38. A telling example is the juxtaposition, within the same narrative context, of analogous experiences from Combray and Venice (3:623–26).

the close of the novel when we are invited to illuminate our own experience through a process of translation and introspection.

The frames of reference that take us beyond the hero's story emerge only gradually, yet assume a definite shape by the last volume, with its explicit statements. It is only retrospectively, however, that we are fully aware of their hierarchical order. While we make our way through the novel, we are subjected to a rigorous apprenticeship in reading that involves our awareness of shifts of emphasis through intersecting discourses and our participation in a growing network of association and identification. When the coordinates of reading are firmly established, a coherent, plausible world emerges: we now understand why there is a move beyond personal story in this quest for the past, and why narrative and philosophic discourse exist side by side. They do not negate but reinforce each other, since commentary illuminates story, while, in turn, story illustrates and confirms all general claims. Such built-in reinforcements make for a tightly knit discourse that becomes more and more persuasive as we go on reading. Everything, as has been shown through story, discourse, and our own reading experience, manifests itself in time. Complete insight is not gained until the end; truths are learned gradually in and through experience. Why this is so is explained in one of Elstir's early lessons:

> On ne reçoit pas la sagesse, il faut la découvrir soi-même après un trajet que personne ne peut faire pour nous, ne peut nous épargner, car elle est un point de vue sur les choses.

> We do not receive wisdom, we must discover it for ourselves, after a journey through the wilderness which no one else can make for us, which no one can spare us, for our wisdom is the point of view from which we come at last to regard the world. (1:864; translation, 1:923–24)

This is why we must make our way through several thousand pages while being initiated into new ways of seeing and being. Along the way, the narrator maps out for us a many-layered program of reading that reveals itself as a palimpsest: inscribed into the autobiographical quest are various models for reading—including Swann's life, the work of several artists, and the narrator's corrective, higher reading. Finally, we begin to see Proust's novel as an allegory of reading when the protagonist turned writer directs us to our own search by offering his work as a model for introspection and artistic creation.[39]

39. Volker Roloff has shown that reading as aesthetic experience was one of Proust's central preoccupations from the time of the first notebooks. He traces, within Proust's writings, "the conception of an exemplary and paradigmatic reading situation illustrating and analyzing at once the reading process as a form of perception and aesthetic communication" ("Lecture et Intertextualité: À propos de l'évolution du discours esthétique dans les *Cahiers* et dans *A la recherche du temps perdu*," *Bulletin d'Informations Proustiennes* no. 13 [1982]: 38, my translation).

F I V E

Toward a Reflexive Act of Reading: Robbe-Grillet's
Projet pour une révolution à New York

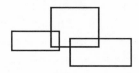

En réalité, chaque lecteur est, quand il lit, le propre lecteur de soi-même.—
MARCEL PROUST, *A la recherche du temps perdu*

Among Robbe-Grillet's novels to date, none has received more attention or provoked stronger reactions than *Projet pour une révolution à New York*. What captures our attention is not so much the author's transgressive narrative practice, to which readers of the *nouveau roman* are accustomed by now,[1] but, rather, the novel's insistent focus on sado-erotic scenes of aggression in which women are victimized. To help the startled reader naturalize the unnatural practices displayed in his novel, Robbe-Grillet, in the explanatory flyer inserted in the book, offers one model for reading by pointing out that the themes generating his text are modern myths that he intentionally displays and plays with, rewriting them in an effort to

---

1. What was once overtly transgressive in its intentional disregard of all conventions gradually becomes more accessible through repeated exposure. The lesson we have learned from reading the *nouveau roman* is that narrative strategies, however unconventional, can be learned. For a discussion of the avantgarde as an evolving concept, with Robbe-Grillet as one example, see Susan Rubin Suleiman, "The Question of Readability in Avant-Garde Fiction," *Studies in Twentieth-Century Literature* (1981–1982): 17–35.

free himself from their grip.[2] But what about those readers who do not catch on to the rules of the game, and who, instead of being freed from the novel's erotic myths, are unduly disturbed by them? The author himself explained how such "misreadings" may come about during an interview focusing on the erotic content of his works. Like other stereotypes inscribed in his fiction, erotic myths, he says, are part of the fragments he detaches from social discourse in order to construct something new. Readers who do not recognize the reworked myths for what they are fall prey, he claims, not to his writing but to the cultural prejudices they bring to their reading:

> In society's discourse, these [fragments] are concepts, but I detach them from their context, take them as building blocks, I push them back to the status of signifiers in order to build another language, which is my own. But society's ideology is so strong that the reader, coming upon these detached concepts, re-establishes their ideological context, and as a result, falls victim, not to *my* ideology, but to *his own*.[3]

What Robbe-Grillet describes here is an instance of conflicting frames of reference: while the writer offers the reader a new frame of reference by recontextualizing stereotypes, the reader thwarts this effort by bringing back into the reading the old system of reference built on cultural conventions—a case not unlike the seventeenth-century reading of *La Princesse de Clèves*. Michael Riffaterre gives a similar explanation for the reader's ideological entrapment by a taboo subject in his discussion of what happens in reading Sade: "The code remains

2. The inserted text that now stands as a preface to the book was originally published in article form in *Le Nouvel Observateur*, 26 June 1970.
3. This interview, conducted by Germaine Brée, has the provocative title, "What Interests Me is Eroticism," and was published in *Homosexualities and French Literature*, ed. George Stambolian and Elaine Marks (Ithaca: Cornell University Press, 1979), pp. 87–100. The quotation above appears on p. 93.

powerful enough to tempt the analyst to mix reading and empirical psychology."[4] Riffaterre shows how, in the case of Sade, "mythography" outweighs pornography, since sequence of synonyms repeats the same meaning, like poetic language,[5] but the reading is not as clear-cut in the case or Robbe-Grillet; here, in addition to struggling with a taboo subject, the reader has to make his way through a labyrinthine narrative discourse whose frame of reference constantly changes, depriving him of all formal, temporal, and causal coherence.[6]

Given the difficulties the novel presents in both form and content, it is not easy to locate the reader's position or to determine his response. Moreover, a lot depends on *who* the reader is: not only must attention be paid to the provocative subject matter, the fragmented narrative form, and the internalized cultural text but also to the personal prejudices that are brought to bear on the reading of the novel. It is at the intersection of form, content, and reader participation that meaning takes place. Each one of these constitutes an important frame of reference that comes into play in the course of a reading. Both the calculated effect of the text on the reader and the reader's disposition during any one reading make up the structures of response.[7] To emphasize how these frames of ref-

4. Michael Riffaterre, "Sade, or Text as Fantasy," *Diacritics* 2 (1972): 9. Sade and sadism in general are obvious intertexts in *Projet*.

5. Ibid., p. 9.

6. *Projet* thus denies the reader all basic narrative functions. What these basic functions are is described by Gérard Genette in "Discours du récit," pp. 261–65. I mentioned Genette's study in Chapter One (p. 5) where I briefly discuss the various functions. How the absence of such narrative functions undermines the text's authority is discussed by Lubomir Doležel in "Truth and Authenticity in Narrative," pp. 7–26. He describes the progressive "destruction of authentication authority" in the evolution of fictional narrative (p. 21). His basic thesis is that "narrative worlds as systems of fictional facts are constructed by the speech acts of the authoritative source—narrator in the broadest sense." He goes on to show how in conventional narrative "procedures of authentication are a fundamental component of the narrative structure" (pp. 23–24).

7. Different critics have studied the interplay between textual structures and

erence jointly function in a poetics of reading, I shall give equal attention to textual features and structures of response in the discussion that follows.

Given the book's provocative subject matter, it is worth asking if and to what extent women read and respond differently than men. Some critics have claimed that *Projet* is primarily a man's book.[8] Yet this claim is exclusively based on two aspects of the text, the repeated scenes of violence with male aggressors and female victims, and the repeated appropriation of the narrative by an inscribed male narrator. To back up her view of the narrator's assertiveness, Susan Suleiman brings in a quotation from Barthes, cogent in its succinct, categorical language: "The master is he who speaks, who has all of language at his disposal; the object is he who remains silent."[9] Yet the same quotation can be used on the reader's behalf if as much attention is paid to the "erotics of form" as to the erotic happenings in the fictional world.[10] Then it becomes possible to account for the reader's active participation in this text and to show that neither male nor female readers need be passive or

reader response, including Michel Charles (*Rhétorique de la lecture*) and Wolfgang Iser (*The Act of Reading*), whose theories are discussed above in the Introduction. More recently, Anselm Haverkamp has studied the aesthetic orientation of texts and the disposition of readers to determine their combined role in setting up "the structures of exchange" (*Transferstrukturen*) of a reading. See the discussion of "Illusion und Empathie" in Chapter One, above.

8. One of the most persuasive arguments for this view is Susan Suleiman's in "Reading Robbe-Grillet: Sadism and Text in *Projet pour une révolution à New York*," *Romanic Review* 68 (1977): 57–59.

9. Ibid., p. 57. The quotation from Barthes comes from his *Sade, Fourier, Loyola* (Paris: Seuil, 1971), p. 36, my translation.

10. Critics of quite different persuasions have begun talking about the "erotics of form." Ground-breaking in this regard was, of course, Barthes's *Le Plaisir du texte*. Freud's writings have been another source; for instance, Peter Brooks draws on Freud's 1908 essay on "Creative Writers and Daydreams" to show how postponement, anticipation, and ambiguation in the telling of a fantasy increase the listener's or reader's pleasure ("On the Possibility of a Psychoanalytic Criticism," talk delivered at the MLA Convention on 28 December 1984). In quite another context, Hans Robert Jauss introduces the concept of "enjoyment through identification," which I shall take up later on in this chapter.

victimized. On the contrary, a close look at the narrative and possible responses to it reveals that in more ways than one the text invites the reader's active participation.

That this novel is a lesson in reading actively is apparent from the very beginning, once we take a close look at how this frame of reference is set up through narrative clues, textual strategies, and reading models. To alert us to the make-believe, fictional nature of the text we are about to embark on, a significant clue is given in the very first paragraph. Instead of guiding us into a fictional universe through a narrative discourse that gradually sets up the expected story coordinates, the novel's opening involves us in another kind of discourse, one that has a definite distancing effect, since it is a passage of metacommentary that presents the fictional universe as repeated, ritualistic role playing:

> La première scène se déroule très vite. On sent qu'elle a déjà été répétée plusieurs fois: chacun connaît son rôle par coeur. Les mots, les gestes se succèdent à présent d'une manière souple, continue, s'enchaînent sans à-coup les uns aux autres, comme les éléments nécessaires d'une machinerie bien huilée.[11]

> The first scene goes very fast. Evidently it has already been rehearsed several times: everyone knows his part by heart. Words and gestures follow each other in a relaxed, continuous manner, the links as imperceptible as the necessary elements of some properly lubricated machinery.

Nor are we likely to forget this code of reading, since the narrator repeatedly refers to his creations in theatrical terms— *scène, action, rôle, personnage, pièce* (scene, action, role, charac-

---

11. *Projet pour une révolution à New York* (Paris: Les Editions de Minuit, 1970), p. 7. The English translation that follows is from *Project for a Revolution in New York*, trans. Richard Howard (New York: Grove Press, 1972), p. 1. Hereafter, unless otherwise specified, page references to both these sources are given sequentially within parentheses. Parenthetical references to only one of these sources are to the French edition.

ter, play)—and since his fictional world is one of constant disguise where characters and narrator play several roles. There is a further warning about reading too literally when the narrator, early in the novel, introduces the idea of *l'acte métaphorique* (p. 38) while describing a scene in which revolutionaries are trained by watching three actors engaged in an ideological debate on rape, arson, and murder—the very acts of violence encountered throughout the novel. The metaphorical enactment of violence, with its emphasis on role playing, may well serve as a reading model for the text we have in front of us: "un dialogue préfabriqué entre trois personnages chargés tour à tour des questions ou des réponses et qui échangent leur rôle par une permutation circulaire à chaque articulation du texte, c'est-à-dire toutes les minutes environ"[12] ("a prefabricated dialogue between or among three persons assigned alternately questions and answers, changing parts by a circular permutation at each shift of the text--i.e., about every minute") (p. 37; translation, p. 27). The full implications of the theater code, which introduces and frames our reading, are quite obvious by the end of the book where once again, in the last paragraph, we are reminded of the ludic, ritualistic nature of the text: "Et brusquement l'action reprend, sans prévenir, et c'est de nouveau la même scène qui se déroule, très vite, toujours identique à elle-mème" ("And suddenly the action resumes, without warning, and it is the same scene which proceeds all over again, very fast, always just as it was before") (p. 214; translation, p. 182). Such commentary and role models, by insisting on the arbitrary, repetitive nature of the text, definitely put the reader on his guard, suggesting, even insisting, that he,

12. all characters in the novel are subject to stereotyping, and, like the roles of these actors, theirs are interchangeable. For instance, in the case of women, as Ann Jefferson has pointed out, "the text merges the masks under the uniform stereotype of the female victim of the sado-erotic" (*The Nouveau Roman and the Poetics of Fiction* [Cambridge: Camridge University Press, 1980], pp. 95–96).

too, play more than one role. Though the theater code is the first and most important guideline in setting up a more self-conscious, critical reading, it is seconded by various narrative techniques and built-in reading models that repeatedly under-score the literariness of the text, making it obvious that its in-tent is poetic, not pornographic. This does not mean that the book's sadism and violence can be dismissed. These aspects are powerful and cannot be denied as an important dimension of the reading, yet they must be viewed within the global con-text where they are set against other frames of reference.

The interplay of narrative form, subject matter, and the reader's disposition may best be shown by a sequential exami-nation of an early segment of the text. A telling example is the novel's first narrative sequence, which is abruptly introduced in the third paragraph, in the midst of the long preamble on role playing that opens the novel. It is certainly significant that the sentence immediately preceding this sequence reads: "Et brusquement l'action reprend, sans prévenir, et c'est de nou-veau la même scène qui se déroule, une fois de plus . . . Mais quelle scène?" ("And suddenly the action resumes, without warning, and the same scene occurs again . . . But which scene?") (p. 7; translation, p. 1). This last question by an uni-dentified voice dramatizes for the reader a possible audience or reader response, thus making him aware of the structures of exchange between reader and text. Without any transition, the next sentence begins, in first-person narration, the account of the first sado-erotic scene: a character dressed like a physi-cian injects a tied-up, naked woman with an unidentified sub-stance. The narrator, in the position of an uninformed out-sider, a voyeur peeking through a window, reveals himself as part of the story world. From his restricted position he can give the reader only partial information and can provide no definite explanation as to what is going on. Yet the hypotheses he offers are enough to set the reader's imagination to work. For example, he takes various guesses at how the helpless woman may have been overpowered, and he jumps to the conclusion that this is possibly a case of artificial insemination or, in any case, an experiment of a monstrous nature (p. 10).

By presenting the scene as an enigma, the narrator mystifies us and holds us in suspense. This heightens our interest in the plot, and encourages us—following the narrator's example— to fill in the blanks. It is at such points in the reading process that we are most likely to be caught in *l'illusion de réel*—not only because our active participation in the fiction-making process makes the story seem more real,[13] but also because the detailed description of the helpless woman, stared at by male characters, narrator, and reader alike, sets up an archetypal scene for fantasies of domination and victimization. Depending on the kind of response set in motion—at this level of reading there is quite a range of possible responses—we are free to experience the scene vicariously or to keep at a safe distance, kept there by a gut reaction of fear or disgust, or by a more critical reaction based on cultural conditioning—such as a feminist reading of the scene. Yet all of these reactions are based on the assumption that there is something "real" about this scene that corresponds to what we experience in the world we live in. The reader is thus easily subject to referential illusion. Such illusions and the responses they call forth are an integral part of reading, as Anselm Haverkamp has shown in his theory of reading based on empathy. Central to his theory is the process through which structures of identification or transference are set in motion during the act of reading.[14] In this context, he singles out empathy as the basic hermeneutic operation necessary to bring about illusions created through literary

13. For a detailed description of the reader's role in filling in the blanks, see Wolfgang Iser's "Indeterminacy and the Reader's Response in Prose Fiction," in *Aspects of Narrative*, ed. J. Hillis Miller (New York: Columbia University Press, 1971), pp. 1–45. According to Iser, indeterminacy is caused, on the one hand, by the reader's lack of identification with the fictional world and, on the other, by formal conditions of the text.
14. Anselm Haverkamp, "Illusion und Empathie."

fiction.[15] Empathy, he explains, sets up a reflexive, participatory reading during which structures of exchange or transference depend on the interrelationship between certain roles inscribed in the text and the disposition of the reader.[16] He specifies that the connection between these two poles is based on the reader's perception of an analogy. This way the reader is no mere onlooker but an active participant, both in setting up the reading process and in setting in motion analogies between aesthetic experience and his own life. Reading, seen from this perspective, becomes an occasion for further self-awareness, a view not unlike that of Roland Barthes, who claims that there is *co-existence* "whenever the 'literary' text (the book) transmigrates into our life, whenever another writing (the writing of the Other) manages to write fragments of our own dailyness."[17]

In taking a closer look at how empathy or reading reflexively works in *Projet*'s sado-erotic scenes,[18] we may well wonder if there is likely to be a radical difference between the reactions of male and female readers. How are we to take, for instance, the description, in the novel's initial scene, of the naked woman's body and her vulnerable position? It is a classic scene of scopophilia, the erotic pleasure derived from looking at another person as an object.[19] The narrator is obviously in the position of peeping Tom, while descriptive detail reveals the

15. Ibid., p. 6.
16. Ibid., p. 3.
17. *Sade, Fourier, Loyola*, p. 12, my translation. A similar view of reading as self-awareness, as an experience that enables the reader to restructure what he already knows, is described in some detail by Wolfgang Iser in *The Act of Reading*, pp. 129–59. For a discussion of this part of Iser's book, see above, Chapter One, p. 9.
18. Empathy is not to be taken, in the narrow sense, as straightforward identification. As Haverkamp points out, ironic as well as humorous control of empathy are possible variants of reader response ("Illusion und Empathie," p. 6).
19. Freud discusses scopophilia in *Three Essays on Sexuality* and "Instincts and their Vicissitudes."

extent of his gaze and his narrative move from passive contemplation to active sadism.[20] By taking this narrative direction
he dramatically emphasizes the male-female opposition and
reinforces the sexual connotations. Laura Mulvey, who has
studied aspects of visual pleasure in the cinema, provides a
useful model for studying audience response to the representation of passive, vulnerable women.[21] The viewer derives
pleasure, she argues, through two structures of looking: (1)
scopophilia, "the pleasure of taking other people as objects,
subjecting them to a controlling and curious gaze[22] and (2)
identification with the image seen, brought about "through
the spectator's fascination with and recognition of his like,"[23]
which, in Freudian terms, is a function of ego libido. While
this structure of response seems plausible for male viewers, it
is more problematic when applied to female spectators or
readers. For instance, if this model is applied to *Projet*, we see
that the female reader, if she is to derive narcissistic pleasure,
has to do some intensive role playing and masquerade as a
male spectator. If she identifies with the victimized woman,
her response is masochistic. Or is she likely to remain ambiv-
alent, oscillating between two opposing roles or refusing to
play any role whatsoever while remaining at a safe distance?

20. Laura Mulvey, drawing on Freud, shows how voyeurism is associated
with sadism in the classic scenarios of narrative films where the voyeur (male)
spies on the woman to ascertain her guilt and punish her accordingly ("Visual
Pleasure and Narrative Cinema," in *Women and the Cinema: A Critical Anthology,* ed. Karyn Kay and Gerald Peary [New York: Dutton, 1977], p. 14. It might
be argued that in this particular narrative situation sadism is needed to get the
story going, since contemplation yields no narrative. Cf. Gérard Genette's
"Vraisemblance et motivation" for a similar functionalist approach to narrative.
21. Mulvey, "Visual Pleasure and Narrative Cinema," pp. 6–18. Mulvey
shows how mainstream films, as one of the influential symbolic orders of
Western society, have helped to perpetuate the image of the passive woman
as object of the male gaze.
22. Ibid., p. 8
23. Ibid., p. 10.

It may be argued that whatever the case, she is confronted with the scene of her own unmaking, either by gazing at it or by participating in it vicariously. It could also be argued that whatever one's view on such responses to the sado-erotic scenes may be, the central position of the reader—male or female—is that of voyeur, and that this position is basically a male position.[24]

Putting theory to the test by surveying actual readers reveals that individual responses to the novel's sado-erotic scenes are quite varied, and do not fall neatly into categories predictable by gender.[25] It also reveals that, whether men or women, we are ultimately involved in the book as active, not passive, readers. Such active reader participation is inscribed in the narrative program of *Projet* through various illusion-breaking techniques that have a distancing effect, calculated to free the reader from the grips of the story and the myths it perpetuates and to ask him to view them critically by making them the object of contemplation.[26] By asking the reader to focus on dis-

24. Laura Mulvey holds this view in her discussion of narrative films in "Visual Pleasure and Narrative Cinema."

25. My information is based on class discussions and papers by undergraduate and graduate students at Brown University. From these I learned that some men identified with the female victims and felt the same kind of malaise as did women who identified with the victims. A few women identified with the aggressor; others identified with neither victim nor aggressor and kept at a "safe" distance, never giving in to the illusion-making passages. Some of these responses were obviously conditioned by a feminist reading in which a strong ideological position thwarted at once the illusionary effects of erotic stereotypes. Varied reader response to *Projet* by critics and literary scholars is discussed in an article by Daniel P. Deneau entitled "Bits and Pieces Concerning One of Robbe-Grillet's Latest Verbal Happenings: The 'Sado-Erotic' *Projet*," in *Twentieth-Century Literature* 25 (1979): 37–53. The author shows how reactions to the book range from ignoring the sado-erotic to moralizing about it or extolling it as therapeutic, cathartic, or imaginative.

26. The rhetorical dimension of reading is the focus in, for example, Michel Charles's *Rhétorique de la lecture*, Wolfgang Iser's discussion of the role of the "implied reader" in *The Act of Reading*, Michael Riffaterre's *Semiotics of Poetry*, and Umberto Eco's discussion of the "Model Reader" in *The Role of the Reader*. All of these are briefly discussed above, in the Introduction.

course and on the fictionality of all symbolic orders, the text invites him to a level of reading that takes him beyond myths and fantasy, and beyond narcissism and masochism. Given such a reading of *Projet*, we are likely to oscillate in our response between being drawn in by the illusion-building passages of erotic violence and distanced by the illusion-breaking narrative strategies through which the text parodies its own fictionality and the reader's vulnerable response to it.

As has been noted, such a critical, dialogic reading is encouraged from the start through the metaphor of role playing. Two paragraphs later, in the midst of the erotic description of the bound woman, the reader is subtly reminded of this frame of reading by a brief illusion-breaking remark: "comme d'habitude, semble-t-il" ("as usual, it would seem") (p. 8; translation, p. 1). What is even more striking, a few lines earlier, is how the narrator, without any transitional warning or break in syntax, slides from the description of the door to the scene of the imprisoned woman, so that the reader can no longer be sure if the narrator is describing an imaginary scene inspired by the peculiar texture of the door made out of imitation wood, or whether he has jumped from the contemplation of one to the other without giving a cue. Given such uncertainty, the reader may begin questioning the existence of both the door and the erotic scene, especially in the context of the theatrical staging set up at the start of the novel. Once again, more than one reading is possible, and it is precisely through such unmarked narrative boundaries that the narrator invites the reader to participate in the writing of the text:

> La surface du bois, tout autour, est recouverte d'un vernis brunâtre où des petites lignes plus claires, qui sont l'image peinte en faux-semblant de veines théoriques appartenant à une autre essence, jugée plus décorative, constituent des réseaux parallèles ou à peine divergents de courbes sinueuses contournant des nodosités plus

sombres, aux formes rondes ou ovales et quelquefois même triangulaires, ensemble de signes changeants dans lesquels j'ai depuis longtemps repéré des figures humaines: une jeune femme allongée sur le côté gauche et se présentant de face, nue de toute évidence puisque l'on distingue nettement le bout des seins et la toison foncée du sexe.

The wood around the window is coated with a brownish varnish in which thin lines of a lighter color, lines which are the imitation of imaginary veins running through another substance considered more decorative, constitute parallel networks or networks of only slightly divergent curves outlining darker knots, round or oval or even triangular, a group of changing signs in which I have discerned human figures for a long time: a young woman lying on her left side and facing me, apparently naked since her nipples and pubic hair are discernible. (p. 8; translation, pp. 1–2)

The only hint, if we catch it, is the narrator's self-conscious reference to his own interpretive activity ("ensemble de signes changeants"), which, in turn, may lead us—depending on how quickly we catch on at this early stage of our reading—to a more self-conscious reading.

We are kept at a critical distance when the narrator, at the end of this scene, reminds us that it is repeatedly played, that everyone has mastered his part so that everything runs like a well-oiled machine (p. 11). In addition to inserting such disconcerting commentary, the narrator does his best to mislead us through narrative discourse. For one thing, we are unable to pinpoint his position in the story world. In one paragraph he leaves the house, in the next he enters it. This zigzag movement between inside and outside scenes is disconcerting, since there are no transitional markers. Whether we rationalize such narrative practice as a cut-up, scrambled sequence or as a quick succession of incomplete scenes never allowed to grow into a coherent story, we cannot help but be aware of the made-up, arbitrary nature of the text. This impression is reinforced when the narrator blatantly contradicts himself: "J'ai oublié ma clef à l'intérieur et je ne pourrai plus rouvrir la porte pour rentrer chez moi. C'est faux, comme toujours, mais l'image est toujours aussi forte et précise de la petite clef d'acier poli, demeurée sur le marbre de la console, dans le coin droit, près du bougeoir en cuivre" ("I have forgotten my key inside and I can no longer open the door to get it back. This is not true, of course, but the image is still as powerful of the tiny steel key lying on the right-hand corner of the marble table top near the brass candlestick") (p. 12; translation, p. 5). When the key becomes a mere image, we begin to question once more the representational status of characters and events depicted in this novel. Yet, by highlighting the key—like a clue in a detective story—the narrator draws us into his machinations: by the end of the novel, this key fits into more than one narrative fragment and may be used by the inventive reader to link several scenes.

That the reader moves in the realm of fictional creation is further highlighted when the narrator, who has been describing things in great detail, suddenly refuses to do so by abruptly introducing three unwarranted *etc*.'s: "Son anneau, plat, parfaitement circulaire, est situé à quelques centimètres seulement de la base hexagonale du bougeoir, etc., dont le corps mouluré (gorges, tores, cavets, doucines, scoties, etc.) supporte . . . etc." ("Its flat, perfectly round ring lies only a couple of inches from the hexagonal base of the candlestick, etc., whose ornamental shaft (fillets, tori, cavettos, cymae, scotias, etc.) supports . . . etc.") (pp. 12–13; translation, p. 5). This sudden intrusion of *etc*. could also be read, of course, as the writer's self-ironic awareness of the plethora of descriptive detail and the reader's need for a change in pace.

Other narrative procedures converge with the ones already

cited to hamper illusion building, keeping us at a safe distance. For instance, we cannot really become absorbed in the
story, since the identity of characters and their relationships
are never spelled out and are constantly changing. In the first
twenty pages, for example, we are left to wonder who the narrator is, who Laura is—she is variously described as "young
woman" (p. 15) and "frail adolescent" (p. 18)—and what exactly their relationship is, since the narrator describes her as
sister, companion, prisoner, victim, and spy. Equally uprooting are abrupt changes in narrative discourse. Though the
book starts out in and repeatedly returns to first-person narration, we are by no means safely anchored in the mode and
voice this frame of narration traditionally implies. For example, in the midst of a narrative account of an intimate scene at
home, the narrator, who has been referring to himself in the
first person as Laura's concerned companion, suddenly
switches to the third person while he turns into an aggressor
who takes her by force (pp. 17–19). A paragraph farther on,
Laura trustingly goes to sleep in the arms of the first-person
narrator (p. 19).[27] We may well wonder whether the two are
engaged in role playing or whether the narrator has abruptly
juxtaposed two separate sequences that refer to different
events. It is by raising these kinds of questions while reading
that we participate in the writing of the text instead of complacently settling down in a coherent story and discourse.

Matters are further complicated when secondary narrators
take over considerable portions of the first-person narrative
without any clear line of demarcation, so that the reader
quickly loses sight of who speaks and from which perspec-

---

27. See p. 23 for another switch from first- to third-person narration and p. 73
for the sudden change form *il* to *je* to which the narrator self-consciously calls
the reader's attention: "Agacé par leur manège, le narrateur—disons 'je', ça
sera plus simple—cherche longuement, un peu à l'écart" ("Irritated by their
behavior, the narrator—let's say 'I,' it will be simpler—looks around for a long
time") (translation, p. 57).

tive.[28] Even within the framework of the initial first-person account, there are improbable points of view. For instance, within a short paragraph, perspective suddenly changes from the narrator's anxious thoughts while he is out in the street to an implausible omniscient point of view revealing what Laura is doing and thinking inside the house (pp. 14–15).[29] Such juggling of voices and perspectives is a constant in Robbe-Grillet's narrative practice and requires a corresponding agility on the reader's part.

Instead of complacently sitting back, a reader attentive to such textual play soon finds himself asking all sorts of questions about this provocative text. In fact, such an active, dialogic reading is repeatedly inscribed in the novel in the form of brief dialogues between the narrator and an anonymous listener. While some of these exchanges come out of the blue, others grow out of the narrative situation as part of the various interrogatories to which characters are subjected.[30] The dia-

---

28. These secondary narratives are neither clearly set off from or subordinated to the principal one, nor do they introduce separate story worlds, since they grow out of interrogations to which the characters are periodically subjected. For example, JR takes over as narrator on p. 99 and possibly goes on until about p. 125; in turn, Laura G. takes on the role of narrator on p. 158. Ben Saïd is given credit for a brief episode on p. 166, whereas from p. 177 on, the narrator's story is presented as a dream.

29. See, for example, pp. 23–26 in which the street scene and the episode of the broken window in the house, previously described from the narrator's point of view, are now presented from Laura's perspective. Her imaginary scenes of possible intruders turn, like the narrator's, into actual scenes of violation (pp. 26–28). Even more disconcerting is the uncertain representational status of the whole scene, since Laura and the two intruders are first presented as *deux personnages* (a reminder of the book's initial metaphor of role playing), while a few lines later on the reader is referred to the descriptive detail of a picture (p. 28).

30. The most obvious exchanges between narrator and narratee are on pp. 18–19, 22, 46–48, 65–66, 76–78, 81–84, 188–91, 205, 207, 209. On p. 47, the reader infers from the context that the questioning takes place between the narrator and a superior for whom he has written a report of his activities: "Il achève de noter ce qui l'intéresse dans le rapport que je viens de faire" ("He finishes writing what interests him in the report I have just made") (translation, p. 35). By

logues have one thing in common in that they question what has been recounted; taken together, their combined effect is a self-conscious *mise en question* of the very text we are reading.

One of the most revealing dialogues occurs in the first third of the novel (pp. 76–78) where the anonymous interlocutor's serious questioning of inconsistencies in the preceding narrative account reinforces our own impression that things do not square in the story world. We are also reminded of improbable narrative stances, such as omniscient narration of scenes not witnessed by the first-person narrator: "D'où tirez vous tous ces détails, au sujet du bain, des parfums, de la robe verte, puisque vous dites ne l'avoir pas revue?" ("Where did you get those details, about her bath, her perfume, the green dress, since you say you didn't see her again?") (p. 77; translation, p. 61). The reader, who by this time is already on his guard, is thus further encouraged to question what he reads.

The most telling exchange comes toward the end of the novel where the narrator is questioned about his storytelling technique (pp. 188–91). This passage makes explicit some of the questions readers may by now have asked, while providing some possible answers. Whether these replies are taken as apologetic guidelines or ironic self-commentary, they remind us of what is striking in this novel and display the narrator's self-conscious awareness of his own text. In turn, such narcissistic inscriptions invite the reader to take a more critical stance, to reflect rather than read viscerally. This is particularly evident when the narrator calls attention to the erotic dimension of his tale by inscribing a listener who asks such pointed questions as "N'avez-vous pas tendance à trop insister . . . sur l'aspect érotique des scènes rapportées?" ("Don't you have a tendency to insist too much . . . on the erotic aspect of the scenes you report?") (p. 188; translation, p. 159). The answer,

---

analogy or inference, the reader could construe similar subsequent exchanges as part of a *compte-rendu* and, by extension, view the entire novel as bits and pieces of a written report. This is one of many possible readings.

ironically, is a long list of gruesome details, which the narrator claims to have omitted to spare the reader. Erotic detail is further displayed when the narrator goes on to defend as accurate a list of expressions singled out by his interlocutor as exaggerated: " 'petits seins naissants,' 'fesses charmantes,' 'cruelle opération,' 'pubis charnu,' 'splendide créature rousse,' 'éclatante plénitude,' et même, une fois: 'courbes voluptueuses des hanches' " (" 'unformed little breasts,' 'charming buttocks,' 'cruel operation,' 'fleshy pubic area,' and once even 'voluptuous curves of the hips' ") (p. 188–89; translation, p. 160). If not exaggerated, what these titillating expressions obviously are is highly charged and revealing, disclosing the narrator's personal interest in what he is describing. Besides drawing our attention to the erotic through such self-conscious commentary, the repetition of erotic detail reminds us of the memorable sado-erotic scenes. Each erotic detail repeated here is a metonymic reference to the female victims the reader has encountered before.

Though we are explicitly reminded of the sado-erotic scenes, their status, in both story world and narrative account, is seriously questioned in the ongoing dialogue between narrator and narratee. To the charge that he gives contradictory accounts, the narrator responds that there is more than one sado-erotic scene, and that it is difficult to distinguish one from the other:"c'était un autre jour, un autre médecin et une autre victime. L'insémination contre nature a été opérée, non par le docteur Morgan, mais par un certain docteur M." ("that was another day, another doctor, another victim. The artificial insemination was performed not by Dr. Morgan but by a certain doctor M.") (p. 190; translation, p. 161). While familiar-looking characters and settings may well give us the confidence to string together separate episodes in quest of a coherent narrative, comments like the present one, along with other distancing devices, are likely to guide us to another reading.

That Robbe-Grillet's text inscribes its own reading becomes

more obvious yet when the critical dialogue between the two interlocutors ends with a discussion of the two salient narrative techniques, *reprise* (retake) and *coupure* (cut) (p. 191). By spelling out the principal features of its narrative practice, the text explicitly lays bare the rules of the game—a game that the "rhetorical" reader has been playing all along and whose rules he has tried to discover by inference, as best he could. Having moved partway through the labyrinthine narrative and still immersed in it, we are bound to take the present passage of metacommentary as a reassuring signpost. In retrospect, when we are in a position to evaluate the combined effect of the various dialogues between narrator and narratee, we realize that they are exemplary, that they function as reading models for our own encounter with the text: they teach us to keep at a critical distance, to beware and be aware of unnatural practices—in both story world and narrative discourse.[31]

Another textual strategy, repetition—including both recurring narrative techniques used to tell the story and repeated references to the same or similar scenes and episodes—plays a central role in engaging us in a more active reading. Though there are repetitions in other narratives, they are particularly unsettling in Robbe-Grillet's fiction, not only because they abound in his novels, but also because their purpose escapes us, since they are not anchored in any coherent discourse or stable narrative situation. Worse yet, there is repetition with variation, leaving us to wonder whether the narrator is referring to the same or a different scene, whether things have changed or whether he is simply unreliable. Recognizing repetition implies an active memory on the reader's part. In turn, the dynamics of memory makes for a participatory reading, since memory, once set in motion, triggers a backward scanning of the text and encourages associations between the pres-

31. A retrospective reading thus clarifies the rhetorical dimension of the text and the effect it has on the reader.

ent and earlier passages. Repetition also encourages the formation of interpretive constructs, since emphasis through repetition implies added significance. This working through by the reader of what has been given him takes the reading forward and brings about a process of reflection and construction.[32]

How the text actively involves the reader in its structuring process through memory and association becomes quite obvious when we look closely at one of the more memorable sado-erotic scenes toward the end of the novel. As we begin to read the description of the bound woman held prisoner by a doctor in a white coat (p. 187), we see it at once as a familiar scenario—familiar because we have already encountered a similar situation. The first such *mise en scène* is the very first scene of the novel (pp. 8–11), which, as has been noted, is problematic in more than one way, since the narrator as voyeur is an uninformed outsider with only a partial, possibly distorted, view of the scene, and since the very status of the scene is called into question through the commentary that precedes and follows it, insisting on the repeated, identical role playing of it all (pp. 7, 11). This, too, we may remember, since we have been repeatedly reminded of such role playing, have been told that characters disguise themselves, and, for additional bait, have been given a detailed account of the display window of a boutique that sells paraphernalia for completely changing one's identity, including masks, wigs, breasts, hands, decapitated heads, and the like (pp. 52–55).

Our second encounter with a similar sado-erotic scene is even more problematic than the first, since it is part of a narrative sequence in which the narrator first imagines what

32. For a recent study of the role of memory in the reading process, see Anselm Haverkamp's article "Allegorie, Ironie und Wiederholung," published in *Text und Applikation*, Poetik und Hermeneutik 9 (Munich: Fink Verlag, 1981), pp. 551–65. He defines repetition as "that moment of a reading where memory is brought forth in the act of reading" (p. 561, my translation).

might or could have happened (pp. 85–86), then slides into the mode of actual reporting, giving the impression that what is being described is actually being witnessed (p. 86). More unsettling yet, a few pages later, is the narrator's casual remark, without any helpful transition or explanation, that the scene is depicted on the cover of a detective novel (p. 90). After such disconcerting referential sliding, we can no longer be sure whether a scene described actually happened in the story world or is merely imagined, or whether it is an artifact within the story world that refers us to another level of representation.[33]

When we come across the third version of the memorable scene toward the end of the novel, it inevitably triggers some narrative crossings. We search our memory to compare present details with previous ones, and to the extent that we remember the plight of earlier victims along with all we imagined then as to what might happen, we begin to anticipate once more, pushing the story forward through our own participatory reading. Yet, at the third repetition of the scene, the narrator does his best to tease our memory. When the victimizer is openly identified as Dr. Morgan, we momentarily feel reassured—about our memory and about a certain coherence and continuity in the story world, especially since our attention has repeatedly been drawn to the doctor's questionable underground operations. These multiple lines of reference open up the possibility for connecting various narrative strands. Just as, encouraged by recurring scenes and characters, we gather momentum, expecting further details for fleshing out what is now a familiar sadistic scene, the narrative comes to a long, frustrating halt while the unidentified inter-

33. John Updike, in a review of contemporary French fiction, shrewdly points out that Robbe-Grillet's self-proclaimed intention of coming up with "descriptions whose movement destroys all confidence in the things described" robs his novels of "the credibility as elemental to the art of narrative as stone or metal is to sculpture" (*New Yorker*, 4 November 1967, p. 228).

locutor questions the narrator about his storytelling technique and points out inconsistencies in the narrative (pp. 188–91). Not only is this kind of interruption illusion breaking in that it pulls us out of the story world and puts a stop to our participation in building up the narrative, but it also activates our memory by encouraging a critical backward scanning of the text. Yet even this activity is seriously undermined when the narrator dismisses all talk about inconsistencies by claiming that seemingly similar scenes took place on different days, with another doctor, another victim.

Another kind of repetition, the reappearance of the same scenes or characters on different levels of existence, becomes increasingly disconcerting. One particularly unsettling repetition is the inscription on tape of a story whose characters, situations, and episodes are the same as those of the principal story. What is even more disorienting is that there is no clear line of demarcation between the two. Though the tape is explicitly introduced into the main story as a tape listened to by its characters (p. 63), we lose sight of where the narrator stops telling us what is on the tape and goes on with his own story. Such entanglement is felt most acutely when we come across passages, supposedly taped, that take up a previously described episode by repeating, altering, or continuing it. This is the same kind of referential sliding and *mise en abyme* that we encounter when the narrator suddenly locates the scene involving the victimized woman on the cover of a detective novel. Such fusion and confusion of representational levels definitely undermine the status of the text we are reading. Not only is the fictional universe in question, but so is the narrative discourse in which we are embroiled, since we wonder if there is actually a narrator telling a story, or if he is merely describing or quoting other texts—books, tapes, posters, and the like.

Textual authority is further undermined through another kind of repetition, which is equally disconcerting in its referential uprooting. For example, in several instances, the narrator presents a montage of descriptive details drawn from scenes previously described as separate settings. One of the most striking passages is the one in which he abruptly juxtaposes details from the scene involving the fire escape, the scene in which the imprisoned Laura stands by the broken window, and the one in which Laura (another, the same?) is in the subway (pp. 64–65). Though the narrator thus sets up a network of intratextual references, the reader loses sight of all narrative sequence. What resonates in his memory is these bits and pieces, not any coherent scene or situation. Nor does re-reading help; on the contrary, it makes him aware of the multiple connections and interpretations in what is obviously an open narrative.[34]

Caught in a labyrinth wherever he turns, since all that happens in the story world is highly questionable, as is the narrator's disorienting discourse, the reader is bound to question seriously his own reading practice. Once he realizes that there is no circumscribed story to infer, no coherent discourse to follow, and, hence, no familiar frame of reference to fall back on, the text is open to other kinds of reading. Memory, instead of stringing together similar scenes and episodes, is now likely to be put to work in a more critical, poetic reading as the reader begins to focus on recurring narrative strategies. Instead of building a story, he is bound to scrutinize the discourse and the effect it has on him. Once he begins to read from this perspective, repetitions emerge as ironic *mise en abyme*, pulling him in opposite directions: although he is first given the impression of textual resonance and reinforcement, he is finally left holding a book whose very text refuses to structure itself. Caught in a blatantly discontinuous narrative with memorable repetitions and timely commentaries that begin to

34. See pp. 41–43, 126, and 214 for repeated mention of the fire escape, and pp. 15–16, 23–24 for an earlier description of the broken window. The reader's memory is thus exercised through repeated references to the same scenes, lending further resonance and significance to the scenes in question.

look like clues, the reader soon finds himself reading vertically, looking for possible associations between similar passages. This kind of comparative scanning involves him in a reading that is poetic and self-conscious rather than referential and illusion making. Once he pays attention to textual design, the sado-erotic details lose much of their *effet de réel*, especially when he realizes that violence and pornography are mere pre-texts (pretexts) for a new reading.

Passages that are of central importance in directing us toward a new reading are those in which the narrator analyzes Laura's reading habits and her way of telling a story: "Malgré un ton soudain animé, amusé même, elle donne toujours cette impression de recevoir d'ailleurs des phrases toutes prêtes, dont elle ne peut elle-même que déchiffrer le sens au fur et à mesure qu'elle les prononce à haute voix"[35] ("Despite a suddenly animated, even amused tone, she still gives that impression of receiving from elsewhere her ready-made sentences, whose meaning she herself can decipher only in the course of speaking them aloud") (p. 113; translation, pp. 92–93). The key phrase is "cette impression de recevoir d'ailleurs des

35. The narrator has already criticized Laura's style in an earlier passage: "Ses paroles ne forment jamais un discours continu: on dirait des morceaux découpés que plus rien ne relie entre eux, en dépit du ton appliqué laissant supposer un ensemble cohérent qui existerait au loin" ("Her words never form a continuous discourse: they are like fragments which nothing any longer links together, despite the emphatic tone suggesting a coherent whole which might exist somewhere") (95; translation, p. 77). Her reading habits are equally sporadic, since she reads several books at the same time, going from one to the other without any rhyme or reason, "modifiant donc sans cesse l'ordonnance de chaque volume, sautant de surcroît cent fois par jour d'un ouvrage à l'autre, ne craignant pas de revenir à plusieurs reprises sur le même passage pourtant dépourvu de tout intérêt visible" ("thereby endlessly altering the arrangement of each volume, leaping moreover a hundred times a day from one work to the next, not minding her frequent returns to the same passage nonetheless stripped of any apparent interest") (p. 95; translation, p. 68). This is not unlike the kind of reading to which Robbe-Grillet's text subjects us, except for the fact that we do not have to switch books, since narrative leaps are built right into *Projet*.

phrases toutes prêtes," since this is indeed, here spelled out, the impression we have reading *Projet*. Suspected here of narrative *bricolage* and actually caught at it (p. 116), Laura's storytelling is a model in miniature of the book's narrative practice. The inscribed criticism serves as a built-in interpretive clue, making explicit what readers have already felt.

By calling attention to narration as fabrication and *bricolage*, the narrator calls into question his own procedure. Such parodic self-reflection sets up a new kind of dialogue with the reader, encouraging him to pay attention to *how* things are put instead of getting carried away by what is said or described. Just as the narrator suspects that Laura's story does not refer to anything that actually happened, so the reader begins to suspect that he is being taught a lesson in *trompe l'oeil*. This becomes quite obvious when Laura goes on telling her story about how she fooled the locksmith who was peeking through the keyhole, tricking him into believing that he was witness to a scene of violence by adroitly placing the cover of the detective novel in such a way that the voyeur could not see the book's title or border but only the sadistic scene of the victimized woman (pp. 113–14). This triple *mise en abyme* has a dizzying effect if we pause to think for a moment. First, the narrator openly warns us about the veracity of Laura's story; in turn, the questionable story itself is about fooling someone. We as readers begin to suspect that the narrator is fooling us, that we, too, are prey to misreading.

Yet, although the reader is repeatedly encouraged to go on to a more critical, second-level reading, he is still likely to be subject to a more direct, literal reading in which what he is told is momentarily taken at face value. We have only to consider any one of the novel's striking scenes of violence to see how the reader is subjected to a paradoxical situation in which he oscillates between affective response (gut reaction to the scene) and a more critical reading. A telling example of the reader's paradoxical situation is his experience of reading the "re-enactment" of the locksmith-as-voyeur scene some eighty pages after the warning about Laura's illusion-making *mise en scène*. The focal point of the recurring scene is a big, black, venomous spider, mentioned only in passing in the previous scene but here described in vivid detail (pp. 193, 195–97). Soon the reader's gaze is caught in the web of the elaborately spun-out description, watching the beast land on the victim's body, zigzagging across it, settling down on her left breast, and finally sinking its fangs into her flesh. By this time, most readers are bound to be quite involved, not as innocent bystanders critically reflecting on the scene, but, instead, carried away by the flow of precise detail highlighting the girl's nakedness and her painful, vulnerable position. With scientific precision we are told where the rope is pinching her, where the spider is going, and what exactly it is doing. We are made to "feel" the presence of the spider through precise references to its anatomy and its every move, while each additional threatening detail is calculated to build up suspense. Though the anatomical details alone have enough *effet de réel* to conjure up the ugly beast—"huit pattes griffues," "longs appendices crochus," "les chélicères de l'appareil buccal," "entourés des palpes maxillaires toujours en mouvement," "mâchoires," "crocs à venin" ("eight hairy legs," "long hooked appendices," "the chelicerae of the mouthparts," "surrounded by continually moving maxillary palps," "jaws," "venom fangs") (translation, p. 167)—we are pushed further in our affective response through the narrator's emotionally charged expressions and striking analogies describing the effect the spider has on the victim ("la sensation insupportable d'une décharge électrique qui n'en finirait pas"; "telles les tenailles de fer aux crocs aigus, rougis au feu" ["the unendurable sensation of an endless electrical discharge"; "like the iron pliers with their sharp red-hot hooks"] [translation, p. 166]). Finally, our complete attention is focused on the effect this scene has on its built-in spectator, the gaping locksmith. By drawing attention to the spellbound spectator, by openly calling him a voyeur while commiserating with the hapless victim thus cruelly exposed to the gaze of others (pp. 195–96), the narrator makes us aware of our position in this and similar scenes. Yet we are bound to go on staring, reading viscerally or vicariously—rather than from a detached distance—as we follow the minute description of the poisonous bite, the young girl's spasmodic death, and the voyeur's sudden participation in the scene as he deflowers the victim. While the sadistic connotations of the scene are highlighted through this additional act of violence and violation, so, ironically, is our awareness of the erotic dimension of our reading, dramatically spelled out when the scene's built-in spectator suddenly becomes an active participant.

If we now work out this analogy, we are already at a safe distance. If we do not, we will get there by the end of the paragraph when the locksmith-voyeur-necrophiliac takes off his mask and is identified by the narrator as the real Ben Saïd (p. 198). At this point we are bound to remember all the role playing and references to role playing we have previously encountered, encouraged to keep at a critical distance while wondering what games are being played—not only in the story world, but with us as readers. One thing is certain by now: as readers of *Projet* we, like its characters, are called on to play more than one role, especially once we are aware of our own being-in-the-text—not only as readers making sense of the novel but also as human beings responding to it emotionally.

That one of the roles we are asked to play is to come face to face with our emotional response to the novel is quite evident from the scene just witnessed. Besides such provocative stagings, with their built-in audience reaction, the narrator's or a character's explicit remarks about emotional reactions—in particular, catharsis—to the scenes of violence are suggestive and encourage us to consider our own response to the novel. We come across the first mention of catharsis early in our reading when the narrator introduces an analogy to Greek drama to highlight the cathartic dimension of a television program about the brutal sacrifice of African virgins: "les rituels religieux de l'Afrique centrale . . . rappelant les représentations théâtrales de l'antiquité . . . dans la mise en scène d'une mythologie aussi meurtrière que cathartique" ("the religious rituals of Central Africa . . . suggesting the theatrical performances of antiquity . . . in the staging of a mythology as murderous as it is cathartic") (p. 39; translation, p. 28). As in the scene involving the locksmith-voyeur, we are given an example of audience reaction to the African ceremony when the narrator describes how it affects one of the novel's characters, JR, who is watching the show on television (pp. 79–80). While descriptive details take us back and forth from the paroxysmal movement of the African ritual to the intensification of the viewer's pleasure, we are likely—once made aware of possible reactions to the scene through this kind of mirror effect—to pay more attention to our own response.

We are already well into the novel before we are reminded a second time of the role of catharsis in connection with scenes of violence. In this instance, Dr. Morgan explains to the captured Laura why people are interested in making documentary films for television of actual victims undergoing torture. Such films, he explains, are part of the "série des 'Crimes individuels éducatifs' qui essaie d'opérer une catharsis générale des désirs inavoués de la société contemporaine" ("series of 'Educational Individual Crimes' which tries to effect a general catharsis of the unacknowledged desires of contemporary society") (p. 154; translation, p. 154). It is not difficult for the reader, during such reflective pauses introduced into the story, to work out an analogy to his own reading experience of the novel's scenes of violence. It is also important to recall that we have been encouraged to do so right from the start of the novel, since, in his prefatory remarks, Robbe-Grillet explicitly states that he intentionally inscribed society's most obsessive myths in *Projet* in order to free the reader from their power by demystifying them. This professed project certainly squares with what the narrator and Dr. Morgan say about catharsis. We are thus encouraged in more ways than one to pay attention to emotional response as one of the frames of reference that play an important role in the reading of *Projet*.

Since it is more difficult to talk about such responses than about structures of the text—especially since we are not accustomed to keeping track of them—it is useful to turn to some reader-oriented theories that have paid particular attention to emotional response and have sketched models for apprehending and describing it. In this regard, Hans Robert Jauss's discussion of patterns of identification between reader and fictional heroes is particularly helpful.[36] The different kinds of identification he describes are all based on a back-and-forth movement between reader and text, and exclude both the naive, uncritical merging with a character (too little distance) and the reader's disinterested reflection (too much distance). In Jauss's view, "all aesthetic experience, including primary levels such as admiration or pity, demand an act of distancing" (p. 160). While reading *Projet*, the reader certainly feels such

36. Hans Robert Jauss, *Aesthetic Experience and Literary Hermeneutics*, trans. Michael Shaw (Minneapolis: University of Minnesota Press, 1982), pp. 152–88 (originally published in German under the title *Ästhetische Erfahrung und literarische Hermeneutik* [Munich: Fink Verlag, 1977], vol. 1). Further references are given in parentheses in the text. Jauss discusses five kinds of identification based on how readers experience different heroes (or the absence of heroes) in different contexts. They include (1) associative identification (based on participation in rituals and games); (2) admiring identification (based on imitation or emulation of a perfect hero); (3) sympathetic identification (based on solidarity with an ordinary, suffering hero); (4) cathartic identification with a tragic or besieged hero; and (5) ironic identification (the negation or refusal of identification). Since Anselm Haverkamp's theory of reading—discussed earlier in this chapter—focuses on the process through which structures of identification or transference are set in motion during the act of reading, it, too, would be another useful model for describing catharsis. See also Volker Roloff, "Identifikation und Rollenspiel: Anmerkungen zur Phantasie des Lesers," in *Zeitschrift für Literaturwissenschaft und Linguistik* 6 (1977): 260–76, which I shall discuss in Chapter Six.

distance as he is alternately pulled into and out of text. Through built-in distancing devices, his attention, though momentarily fixed on the sado-erotic scenes, is continually redirected to the text itself as an object of scrutiny and gradually to his own reading and responding. Instead of losing himself in the fictional universe, he is made aware of the myths that delude him and the fabricated nature of both reading and writing. In this respect, the reader's attitude corresponds to what Jauss describes as ideal cathartic behavior: disinterested interest, free reflection, and free judgment (p. 159).

Though a cathartic reading in which the reader is free to contemplate and judge fictional events from a safe distance is part of the experience of reading *Projet*, the novel's predominant pattern of response, given Jauss's categories, is ironic identification. In his view, ironic identification is the norm-breaking pattern par excellence (p. 158), since it "refers to a level of aesthetic reception when an expectable identification is held out to the spectator or reader only to be subsequently ironized" (p. 181). In *Projet*, the reader is not so much teased into "expectable identification" as "shocked into withholding identification" (p. 186), since he is confronted with a world entirely reduced to aggressors and victims.

Another aspect of emotional response that Jauss's theory enables us to describe is the kind of pleasure or enjoyment readers feel when they interact with the text. Jauss emphasizes that this kind of enjoyment is based on "taking part," that it is the enjoyment of the self in and through the enjoyment of what is other" (p. 160). He also points out that during this dialectical exchange, the reader increasingly enjoys both the aesthetic object, which is progressively revealed to him, and his "own self which in this activity feels released from its daily existence" (p. 32). Jauss has some reservations, however, when it comes to modern, avant-garde art and literature, in which, according to him, the only source of aesthetic pleasure that remains is the poetic activity of the spectator or reader, and not the art object itself (p. 187). This kind of poetic reflection, he argues, consists primarily of a questioning reflection during which the startled viewer or reader looks for the possible meaning and importance of the object before him. Such questioning certainly plays an important part in the reading of *Projet*. Yet Jauss imposes unnecessary limits on aesthetic response by favoring traditional literature. To redress the balance, it is useful to turn briefly to Roland Barthes.

Though Barthes, like Jauss, allows for the dialectical play between reader and text that assures enjoyment,[37] he clearly favors unconventional texts. This is obvious from the categorical distinction he makes between *plaisir* (pleasure)—found in texts where the self is able to affirm itself—and *jouissance* (bliss)—felt when the self, lost in the "paradise of words" of the "writerly" text, is negated:

> Text of pleasure: the text that contents, fills, grants euphoria; the text that comes from culture and does not break with it, is linked to a *comfortable* practice of reading. Text of bliss: the text that imposes a state of loss, the text that discomforts (perhaps to the point of a certain boredom), unsettles the reader's historical, cultural, psychological assumptions, the consistency of his tastes, values, memories, brings to a crisis his relation with language.[38]

37. See Roland Barthes, *Le Plaisir du texte* (Paris: Seuil, 1973), p. 11.
38. Ibid., pp. 25–26. The English translation is from *The Pleasure of the Text*, trans. Richard Miller (New York: Hill and Wang, 1975), p. 14. For Barthes's distinction between *texte lisible* (readerly text) and *texte scriptible* (writerly text), see his *S/Z* (Paris: Seuil, 1970), pp. 10–12. Jauss rejects Barthes's categorical distinction because it favors avant-garde literature at the expense of earlier literature (*Aesthetic Experience and Literary Hermeneutics*, pp. 29–30). For the same reason, Jauss opposes Wolfgang Iser's view of worthwhile literature as the communication of "something new" through negation of the existing norm. Though Jauss in his earlier work shared this view, he now believes that the main function of literature is norm-forming, not norm-breaking (pp. xxxviii–xxxix). Jauss ultimately sees Barthes as a philologist: "Since he fails to open the self-sufficient linguistic universe with enough decisiveness toward the world of aesthetic practice, his highest happiness ultimately remains the

Given this view, *Projet* would certainly be a text of *jouissance*.

Some recent studies have shed further light on how the reader's enjoyment is enhanced through certain attention-compelling textual features. Peter Brooks, for instance, examines the "erotics of form" to see to what extent pleasure and desire are determined by such textual strategies as postponement, anticipation, and ambiguation in the telling of a narrative.[39]

By calling attention to the reader's emotional response to literature, such theories provide new frames of reference for reading and talking about *Projet*, and they help account for the strong reactions this novel has provoked. In my own reading and rereading of this novel, enjoyment came from taking charge of the text by paying attention to the interplay between narrative form, sensational subject matter, and the reader's variable disposition and response. Such a reading is by no means an innocent and spontaneous one. It is a highly self-conscious response to a novel whose insistent artifice provoked such a reading. Many other readings are possible. In fact, Robbe-Grillet invites his readers in theory and practice, to impose a new order, their own, on his texts. In his words, "It is the artifice itself which appears on the scene in the novel. And the great advantage . . . even the great didactic advantage, of this operation is to place the reader opposite, so to speak, his own liberty."[40]

By provoking different kinds of responses and by offering us more than one role to play, Robbe-Grillet's novel encourages us to become active participants. Both male and female readers are given this opportunity, since both are free to par-

---

rediscovered eros of the contemplative philologist and his undisturbed preserve: 'the paradise of words' " (p. 30).

39. Peter Brooks outlined this approach to reading in his talk entitled "On the Possibility of a Psychoanalytic Criticism." See also his *Reading for the Plot: Design and Intention in Narrative* (New York: Knopf, 1984).

40. Alain Robbe-Grillet, "Order and Disorder in Film and Fiction," trans. Bruce Morrissette, *Critical Inquiry* 4 (1977): 5.

ticipate or not in this open text. Only those who refuse to play the game are likely "victims," not only because, in Barthes's words, "the master is he who speaks, who has all of language at his disposal; the object is he who remains silent," but also because the passive reader—refusing to take control of the text—is likely to suffer from boredom and frustration, unless, of course, he or she simply abandons *Projet* altogether.

The reader and the critic of Robbe-Grillet's novel are thus faced with the challenge of a new reading without being given a clear itinerary or its full implications. This reading is "new" in that the text encourages a more reflexive—participatory, self-conscious, and critical—reading that sets in motion complex structures of exchange between reader and text. The direction I have taken is to focus on the novel's more visible landmarks, and the more memorable hurdles and gaps, while pausing to consider the different roles the reader is invited to play as well as a range of possible responses. This enabled me to work toward a more complex, "reflexive" (interactive) poetics of reading, including frames of reference based on both textual structures and structures of response.

S I X

Conclusion: New Directions in the Reading of
Narrative Fiction

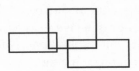

Le plaisir d'une lecture garantit sa vérité.—BARTHES, *Sade, Fourier, Loyola*

What is it to read novels? This is the question asked at the outset of this study. It is clear by now that there is no one simple answer. Readings differ depending on the kind of novel being read and the reader's purpose, interests, and ideology. By opening the interpretive space between reader and text to include both text interpretation and self-interpretation, the frames of reference that come into play are multiplied. Moreover, the emphasis in recent theories of reading on emotional response—in particular the enjoyment readers get from taking an active part—opens up new directions for a poetics of reading.

This excursion through a variety of novels and critical approaches has shown the necessity for broadening the notion of poetics by taking it beyond the study of the internal features of the text to the structures of exchange between text (the printed work) and reader, since the completed, final "text" is constituted in and through the act of reading. Reading reflexively, as Ricoeur, Iser, Haverkamp, and Brooks have shown, opens up texts by constituting them as an event in time, which gives them their ultimate meaning.[1] Reading thus viewed is closely linked to other realms of our experience: for Haverkamp, it is the reader's disposition that actually determines the shape a given reading will take; for Iser, the experience of being in the text has important repercussions on life, since it brings about a restructuring of experience—a view compatible with Brooks's psychoanalytic model of reading based on the dialogic reordering of the life story during transference.[2] Not unlike these views, feminist theory has shown how the reader's identity and experience determine the shape of a particular reading. In discussing such theories, Jonathan Culler points out that "for a woman to read as a woman is . . . to play a role she constructs with reference to her identity as a woman."[3]

Since the reader's experience is an indispensable point of reference, more work needs to be done on a poetics of reading that is truly interactive, focusing as much on the reader as on the text while freeing itself from normative concepts and theories. I have taken a step in that direction by paying attention to the multiple, interlocking frames of reference that come into play in the reading of narrative fiction. Recent scholarship in

1. In addition to Ricoeur's earlier essay "Qu'est-ce qu'un texte?" discussed above in Chapter One, his recent studies on time and narrative give further insight into narration and reading as events in time. See *Temps et récit*, vol. 1 (Paris: Seuil, 1983); vol. 2, *La configuration dans le récit de fiction* (Paris: Seuil, 1984); and vol. 3, *Le temps raconté* (Paris: Seuil, 1985).

2. See Chapter One for a discussion of the theories of reading advocated by Paul Ricoeur, Wolfgang Iser, and Anselm Haverkamp. Peter Brooks draws on Freud, because Freud, according to Brooks, deals with "the 'narratability' of life and the uses of the stories we tell." In Brooks's view, "the narrative text conceived as transference . . . becomes the place of interpretation and construction of the plotted story" (*Reading for the Plot*, p. 320). He goes on to explain that "the psychoanalytic model of remembering is invaluable since it reaches out to include repeating, working through, and reconstructing—all of which seem . . . to characterize the literary text and our reading of it, to define the text-as-read" (p. 321).

3. Culler, *On Deconstruction*, p. 64.

the aesthetics of reception is complementary to my approach. In addition to Iser, Jauss, and Haverkamp, whose theories I have drawn on, Volker Roloff has contributed important insights for studying the interaction between reader and text. He argues for the need to go beyond the work done by some of the prominent scholars in the field of *Rezeptionsästhetik*, since he feels that they have locked themselves in by drawing on certain phenomenological premises, such as the radical distinction between the experience of reading fictional texts and experience in the real world.[4] As a first step toward a more dynamic model of reading, Roloff underlines the importance of studying the process of role playing. This is important, he argues, not only because the reader may accept, reject, or, in different ways, alter the role that is laid down for him in the text (pp. 44–45), but also because the reader is actively involved in imaginary role playing—including such reactions as identification, projection, association building, sympathy, and antipathy (p. 50). Such a "psychodynamic process of reading," Roloff points out, is a "continuous process of associations and adjustments, which depends on the experience and values of each individual recipient" (p. 52, my translation) as well as on his social or historical distance from the text. Roloff views reading as a "complex and tense confrontation" (p. 51), and urges the critic to pay as much attention to the reader's freedom and initiative as to the construct of textual strategies.[5]

To be more specific about the dynamics of role playing, Roloff concentrates on empathy and identification.[6] It is noteworthy that in defining these concepts he turns to Proust and Sartre instead of drawing on the critical tradition in which he

---

4. Volker Roloff, "Der Begriff der Lektüre in kommunikationstheoretischer und literaturwissenschaftlicher Sicht," *Romanistisches Jahrbuch* 29 (1979): 42.

5. Roloff, "Empathie und Distanz—Überlegungen zu einem Grenzproblem der Erzähl- und Leserforschung (am Beispiel von Sartre's *L'Idiot de la famille*)," in *Erzählforschung*, ed. Eberhard Lämmert (Stuttgart: Metzler, 1982), p. 280.

6. See Roloff, "Empathie und Distanz," pp. 269–89, and his "Identifikation und Rollenspiel," pp. 260–76.

was trained. For instance, he faults Jauss for confining his view of identification to the narrow, idealistic conception of identification as "pure, disinterested contemplation of aesthetic works" and praises Proust for his broader understanding of this concept in the framework of a detailed psychology of consciousness.[7] Sartre, on the other hand, is brought in to make the point that empathy is the central concept operative in all understanding.[8] Following Sartre, who views empathy as a combination of identification and critical distance, Roloff redefines empathy as a complex concept including such diverse reactions as sympathy, connivance, and antipathy.[9] In the final analysis, Roloff, like Sartre, views reading as a process of role playing that leads to understanding.[10] In this respect, his concept of reading is close to Haverkamp's theory of empathy and Brooks's theory of transference and backs up my discussion of the structures of exchange in the reflexive reading of Robbe-Grillet's *Projet*, with its emphasis on role playing and catharsis.

Once we consider such new approaches for a poetics of reading, we realize the limits of a strictly formal narratological model. Though Genette's work on narrative is an excellent starting point for locating the salient features of a text, it is confined to analysis within the borders of the text. Genette resolutely refuses, as is evident from his recent *Nouveau discours du récit*, to transgress such textual borders. For instance, in response to Wayne Booth's charge that he does not account for the reader's emotional response, Genette replies that such responses are not the province of narrative discourse: "Our sympathy or antipathy for a character depends primarily on the psychological or moral (or physical!) characteristics with which

7. Roloff, "Identifikation und Rollenspiel," pp. 269–71. See pp. 149–50 above for a discussion of Jauss's patterns of identification.
8. Roloff, "Empathie und Distanz," p. 269.
9. Ibid., p. 270.
10. Ibid., p. 281.

the author endows him, the behavior and speech he attributes to him, and very little on the technique of the narrative in which he figures."[11] Yet the extent to which narrative technique can manipulate the reader is obvious when we remember, for instance, how, through abrupt juxtapositions of contrasting speech and perspectives, we are taken from sympathy to irony in *Madame Bovary*, or how, in Proust's novel, we are repeatedly encouraged to empathize with its characters through the narrator's tendency to open up communication with the reader by taking him from the story world to a more universal discourse. Though Genette admits that certain *effets de focalisation* may well have psychological effects on the reader,[12] he does not include any discussion of the interaction of textual perspectives and the reader's active collaboration in the construction of the text. Contrary to the views held by Iser, Brooks, Haverkamp, and Roloff, Genette concludes, somewhat pessimistically, that reader involvement is unlikely in the modern novel because of the negative effects of innovative technique: "The narrative subtleties of the modern novel, since Flaubert and James, like free indirect discourse, interior monolog or multiple perspective have rather negative effects on the reader's desire to get involved and doubtless contribute to confusing him, to misleading him in his 'evaluations' and to discouraging any kind of sympathy or antipathy."[13]

Though such negative reactions are quite possible within the range of responses to a given novel, the readings in this study of Flaubert, Proust, and Robbe-Grillet—all modern, innovative novelists—opened up other possibilities of response in and beyond the text. We saw, for instance, various ways in which texts inscribe their own theory or practice of reading. In this regard, Proust's novel is exemplary in showing the reader the way through timely interpretive models. To a certain ex-

11. Genette, *Nouveau discours du récit*, p. 106, my translation.
12. Ibid.
13. Ibid.

tent, all of the novels studied here offer the reader one or more models of how they are to be read. At first reading, as we make our way through the novel, we gradually discover such directives through emphasis and repetition; in a retrospective reading, however, their function is quite obvious from the start. Such guidelines are most subtle and indirect in *La Princesse de Clèves* and *Madame Bovary*, whose readers benefit from the models of reading given the characters, and the account of how these characters thrive on them or perish through them. While stories told about love and betrayal constitute a principal frame of reference in *La Princesse de Clèves*, in Flaubert's novel it is Emma's ways of misreading that stand out. Repeatedly faced with these negative versions of reading, we, as readers, in turn begin to question the symbolic orders through which we think and speak, and begin to look more self-critically at our own reading of the text.

The questioning of the text and of the self that subtly begins with *La Princesse de Clèves* and intensifies in *Madame Bovary* and *A la recherche* is at the very center of *Projet*. By self-consciously displaying and working against cultural stereotypes, canons of literary practice, and conventional ways of reading, Robbe-Grillet leads the reader to a frame of mind in which he becomes acutely conscious of the text, the cultural context it undermines, and his own being-in-the-text.

What is the ultimate effect of such self-conscious writing and reading on us as readers of novels? Should we agree with Gerald Graff, who claims that in such metafictional texts the relationship between life and art is seriously undermined? The answer, I think, is somewhat closer to what Linda Hutcheon had to say in response to Graff: "Unlike Gerald Graff, I would not argue that in metafiction the life-art connection has been either severed completely or resolutely denied. Instead, I would say that this 'vital' link is reforged, on a new level—on that of the imaginative process (of storytelling), instead of on that of the product (the story told). And it is the new role of the reader that is the vehicle of this change."[14] It is not only this new focus on narrative process but also the attention now paid to the structures of exchange between reader and text that reforge the link between life and art. In metafiction, it is not merely the text that is self-conscious and self-reflexive, but, through it, also the participating reader.

Opening up the interpretive space between reader and text makes for a more dynamic, flexible poetics of reading. No longer confined to the static structures of the self-sufficient text, such a poetics calls for redefinition of what we understand by "reference," "fiction," and "mimesis."[15] For instance, once we include the reader's actualization of the text, mimesis can no longer be considered as a *re*presentation of a given state of affairs, but rather as a creative construction—bringing in the reader's memory, experience, and role playing—during the act of reading. In recent scholarship, it is Ricoeur who has provided one of the most extensive revisions of the concept of mimesis. In his three-volume study of time and narrative, he introduces the discussion of a "triple mimesis" and specifies the role each level of mimesis plays in the reading of narrative fiction:[16] at the level of mimesis I, it is the reader's familiarity

14. Linda Hutcheon, *Narcissistic Narrative: The Metafictional Paradox* (Waterloo, Ontario: Wilfrid Laurier University Press, 1978), p. 3. See also Gerald Graff's article, "The Myth of the Postmodernist Breakthrough," *Tri-Quarterly* 26 (1973): 383–417.

15. For an up-to-date, intelligent discussion of reference and fiction, in particular, fictional reference, see Catherine Kerbrat-Orecchioni, "Le Texte littéraire: non-référence, autoréférence, ou référence fictionnelle?" *Texte*, no. 1 (1982): 27–49. Her main points, with which I agree and which complement what I said about frames of reference and fiction in Chapter One, are that "every text, in a certain way, refers; 'refers,' that is to say points to a world (pre-structured, or structured by the text itself) placed outside of language" (p. 28) and that "fictionality is a question of degree," since "every text presents itself as a cocktail each time new and unedited, composed of a variable mixture of real and fictional, constructed and preconstructed ingredients" (p. 36, my translation).

16. See Ricoeur, *Temps et récit*, for the discussion of the three levels of mimesis (1:87–129). Further references are given parenthetically in the text. This new concept of mimesis is applied in the next two volumes. Of special interest, in

with the world of action and his knowledge of symbolic systems—in particular, the conventions of narrative discourse—that provide a firm basis for reading (pp. 87–95); mimesis II comprises the internal features of the narrative text and the construction of the plot (p. 103); finally, mimesis III marks, we are told, the intersection between the world of the text and the world of the reader (p. 109). Ricoeur insists that the text does not become a work of art until the moment of interaction between text and reader: "The act of reading is thus the operator that links mimesis III to mimesis II. It is the ultimate vector in the restructuring of the world of action within the framework of the plot" (p. 117, my translation).

Given such new conceptions of text, reference, and mimesis, literature can no longer be considered a special case of language totally separate from the rest of our experience. This is certainly true once we admit that reading novels calls on our experience, is in part fashioned by it, and, in turn, enhances it. Nor can we go on upholding the hierarchical opposition between fact and fiction, serious and nonserious discourse. Moreover, by going beyond formalism to pay attention to the special conditions and assumptions of a particular context of reading, the focus necessarily shifts from the search for fixed meanings to the dynamics of interpretation. Given this new framework, interpretation, as Hilary Putnam so aptly put it, is no longer a matter of right or wrong, but "a conversation with many voices."[17]

Since this view of reading no longer allows for the simplistic view of a stable, objective reference laid down in the text, the new basis for interpretation—its principles and process of discovery—needs to be clarified. I have introduced the model of

---

reference to my reading of *A la recherche*, are two chapters devoted to Proust, the first in *Temps et récit*, 2:194–225, the second in ibid. 3:184–202.

17. From a talk entitled "Is There a Fact of the Matter about Fiction," which was delivered during an MLA Forum on "Fiction and its Referents" on 29 December 1981 in New York.

multiple frames of reference to guard not only against one-sided readings but also against the endless proliferation of meaning. While, like the deconstructionists, I pay attention to both the structures of the text and the structures of reading, my focus is on how meaning is built up—not deferred or thwarted—through the convergence of the particular frames of reference that come into play in a given context of reading.[18] The poetics of reading I have proposed is flexible enough to allow for new frames of reference to be introduced. For instance, I have discussed how some recent theories focusing on emotional response can be incorporated into such a poetics, and how they allow for a wide range of responses. While some theorists pay attention to the "erotics of form"[19] and the enjoyment readers derive from taking an active part in reading, others emphasize the negation and frustration found in those texts that communicate something new.[20] For example, Jauss shows how the reader finds enjoyment through identification in traditional works of literature, while Iser concentrates on how negation and the structure of the blank lead to meaningful communication in modern, avant-garde texts.[21]

18. For an incisive description of where the emphasis lies in a deconstructive approach, the following observation by Jonathan Culler is particularly revealing: "Deconstructive writings will try to put in question anything that might seem a positive conclusion and will try to make their own stopping points distinctively divided, paradoxical, arbitrary, or indeterminate" (*On Deconstruction*, pp. 259–60).

19. See, for example, Peter Brooks's response to Susan Sontag's claim, made some years ago, that we need an "erotics" of art instead of theories of interpretation (Brooks, *Reading for the Plot*, pp. xv, 36). The book to which he responds is *Against Interpretation* (New York: Farrar, Strauss and Giroux, 1966), p. 14.

20. See, for example, Iser, *The Act of Reading*, pp. 53–85. The key statement revealing Iser's view is on p. 69: "Communication always entails conveying something new." He goes on to emphasize that the literary work of art "represents a reaction to the thought system which it has chosen and incorporated in its own repertoire" so that "the result of this operation is the rearranging and, indeed, reranking of existing patterns of meaning" (p. 72).

21. For Iser's discussion of the dynamics of negation and the blank, see *The Act of Reading*, pp. 180–231.

Since a poetics of reading novels should be broad enough to account for both old and new literature as well as for the different aspects of the act of reading—including the dynamics of intertextuality and aspects of narrative discourse—I have found it most fruitful to combine several approaches. How compatible and complementary these theories are in covering the different stages of reading and the range of possible responses I hope to have shown by taking the reader through a variety of novels and critical approaches. Moreover, we should bear in mind that old novels can be given new readings—as Ricardou has shown by applying insights from the New Novel to a reading of Proust—while, conversely, new novels can draw on, and be viewed from familiar frames of reference that help us naturalize them.[22] Since views and theories differ and constantly change, we should realize that "the reader's experience—at least in interpretations—is always a fiction: a narrative construction in a story of reading."[23] The extent to which the construct of a reader reading shapes our reading of fiction and, in turn, our discourse about fiction, is a frame of reference we cannot ignore.[24]

22. Such new readings are discussed by Jean Ricardou in "Proust: A Retrospective Reading," trans. Erica Freiberg, *Critical Inquiry* 8 (1982): 531–41. He points out that "there is a way of enjoying today's literature that gives one a better understanding of the literature of the past" (p. 541), and, one might add, a better understanding of the self.

23. The words are Jonathan Culler's in "Problems in the Theory of Fiction," *Diacritics* (1984): 4.

24. There are quite a variety of such constructs of the reader in contemporary literary theory, including the concepts of the "implied reader"—ranging from networks of response-inviting structures (Iser) to the intentional structures of literary texts (Booth)—the "competent reader" (Culler), the "informed reader" (Fish), the "Model Reader" (Eco), and the "narratee" (Genette, Prince)—the built-in recipient of the narrator's discourse, a mediating figure who, in more ways than one, as Gerald Prince has shown, sets up a line of communication between a narrative text and its actual, "real" readers.

WORKS CITED

Alcorn, Marshall W., and Mark Bracher. "Literature, Psychoanalysis, and the Re-Formation of the Self: A New Direction for Reader-Response Theory." *PMLA* 100 (1985): 342–54.

Anderegg, Johannes. *Fiktion und Kommunikation: Ein Beitrag zur Theorie der Prosa.* 2d ed. Göttingen: Vandenhoeck and Ruprecht, 1977.

Auchincloss, Louis. "Flaubert and James—Opposing Points of View." *New York Times Book Review,* 24 June 1984.

Bakhtin, M. M. *The Dialogic Imagination.* Ed. Michael Holquist. Austin: University of Texas Press, 1981.

Bal, Mieke. *Narratologie.* Paris: Klincksieck, 1977.

Banfield, Ann. "The Formal Coherence of Represented Speech." *PTL* 3 (1978): 289–314.

Barthes, Roland. "L'Effet de réel." *Communications* 11 (1968): 84–89.

———. "From Work to Text." In *Textual Strategies,* ed. Josué V. Harari, pp. 73–81. Ithaca: Cornell University Press, 1979.

———. "Historical Discourse." In *Introduction to Structuralism,* ed. Michael Lane, pp. 145–55. New York: Basic Books, 1970.

———. "An Introduction to the Structural Analysis of Narrative." *NLH* 6 (1975): 237–72.

———. *Le Plaisir du texte.* Paris: Seuil, 1973.

———. *The Pleasure of the Text.* Trans. Richard Miller. New York: Hill and Wang, 1975.

———. *Sade, Fourier, Loyola.* Paris: Seuil, 1971.

———. *S/Z.* Paris: Seuil, 1970.

Benveniste, Emile. *Problèmes de linguistique générale.* Paris: Gallimard, 1966.

Bleich, David. *Subjective Criticism.* Baltimore: Johns Hopkins University Press, 1978.

Booth, Wayne. *A Rhetoric of Irony*. Chicago: University of Chicago Press, 1975.

Bray, René. *Formation de la doctrine classique*. Paris: Nizet, 1927.

Brooks, Peter. "On the Possibility of a Psychoanalytic Criticism." Talk delivered at the MLA Convention, 28 December 1984 in Washington, D.C.

———. *Reading for the Plot: Design and Intention in Narrative*. New York: Knopf, 1984.

Chamard, Henri, and Gustave Rudler. "La Couleur historique dans *La Princesse de Clèves*." *Revue du XVIème Siècle* 5 (1917): 1–20; 231–43.

———. "Les Sources historiques de *La Princesse de Clèves*." *Revue du XVIème Siècle* 2 (1914): 92–131; 289–321.

Charles, Michel. *L'Arbre et la source*. Paris: Seuil, 1985.

———. *Rhétorique de la lecture*. Paris: Seuil, 1977.

Charleton, D.G. "The Language of Disorder." *TLS*, 6 December 1974, p. 1391.

Cogman, P.W.M. "Reading a Painting by Elstir." *French Studies* 30 (1976): 419–32.

Cohn, Dorrit. *Transparent Minds: Narrative Modes for Presenting Consciousness in Fiction*. Princeton: Princeton University Press, 1978.

Cohn, Dorrit, and Gérard Genette. "Nouveaux nouveaux discours du récit." *Poétique* 61 (1985): pp. 101–109.

Cordesse, Gérard. "Note sur l'énonciation narrative." *Poétique* 65 (1986): 41–46.

Crosman, Inge. "Metaphoric Function in *A la recherche du temps perdu*." *Romanic Review* 67 (1976): 295–99.

———. *Metaphoric Narration: The Structure and Function of Metaphors in "A la recherche du temps perdu"*. Chapel Hill: University of North Carolina Press, 1978.

———. "Reference and the Reader." *Poetics Today* 4 (1983): 89–97.

———. "The Status of Metaphoric Discourse: Paul Ricoeur: *La Métaphore vive*." *Romanic Review* 68 (1977): 207–16.

Culler, Jonathan. *Flaubert: The Uses of Uncertainty*. Ithaca: Cornell University Press, 1974.

———. *On Deconstruction: Theory and Criticism after Structuralism*. Ithaca: Cornell University Press, 1982.

———. "Problems in the Theory of Fiction." *Diacritics* 14 (1984): 2–11.

———. *The Pursuit of Signs: Semiotics, Literature, Deconstruction*. Ithaca: Cornell University Press, 1981.

———. *Structuralist Poetics*. Ithaca: Cornell University Press, 1975.

Dällenbach, Lucien. "Intertexte et autotexte." *Poétique* 27 (1976): 282–96.

DeJean, Joan. "Lafayette's Ellipses: The Privileges of Anonymity." *PMLA* 99 (1984): 884–902.

de Man, Paul. *Allegories of Reading: Figural Language in Rousseau, Nietzsche, Rilke, and Proust*. New Haven: Yale University Press, 1979.

———. *Blindness and Insight: Essays in the Rhetoric of Contemporary Criticism*. New York: Oxford University Press, 1971.

Deneau, Daniel P. "Bits and Pieces Concerning One of Robbe-Grillet's Latest

Verbal Happenings: The 'Sado-Erotic' *Projet.*" In *Twentieth-Century Litera-ture* 25 (1979): 37–53.

Doležel, Lubomir. "Truth and Authenticity in Narrative." *Poetics Today* 1 (1980): 7–26.

Doubrovsky, Serge. "*La Princesse de Clèves*: une interprétation existentielle." *La Table Ronde*, no. 138 (1959): 36–48.

Duchet, Claude. "Avant-Propos." In *Le Réel et le texte*, pp. 7–9. Centre de Re-cherches Dix-Neuviémistes de l'Université de Lille III. Paris: Armand Colin, 1974.

Eco, Umberto. *The Role of the Reader: Explorations in the Semiotics of Texts.* Bloom-ington: Indiana University Press, 1979.

———. *A Theory of Semiotics.* Bloomington: Indiana University Press, 1976.

Ferraris, Denis. "Quaestio de legibilibus aut legendis scriptis: Sur la notion de lisibilité en littérature." *Poétique* 43 (1980): 282–92.

Ferraris, Maurizio, and Daniela de Agostini. "Proust, Deleuze et la répétition: Notes sur les niveaux narratifs d'*A la recherche du temps perdu.*" *Littérature*, no. 32 (1978): 66–85.

Fish, Stanley. "How to Do Things with Austin and Searle: Speech Act Theory and Literary Criticism." *MLN* 91 (1976): 983–1025.

———. *Is There a Text in This Class?* Cambridge, Mass.: Harvard University Press, 1980.

Flaubert, Gustave. *Madame Bovary.* Paris: Garnier-Flammarion, 1966.

———. *Madame Bovary.* Trans. Paul de Man. New York: W. W. Norton, 1965.

Fontenelle, Bernard le Bovier. Letter published in *Le Mercure Galant*, May 1678, pp. 111–28.

Foucault, Michel. "The Order of Discourse." In *Untying the Text*, ed. Robert Young, pp. 48–78. Boston: Routledge and Kegan Paul, 1981.

Freud, Sigmund. *Complete Psychological Works.* Ed. James Strachey. 24 vols. London: Hogarth, 1953–1974.

Gadamer, Hans Georg. *Wahrheit und Methode.* Tübingen: Mohr, 1965.

Genette, Gérard. "Discours du récit." In *Figures III.* Paris: Seuil, 1972.

———. "Frontières du récit." In *Figures II*, pp. 49–69. Paris: Seuil, 1969.

———. *Narrative Discourse: An Essay in Method.* Trans. Jane E. Lewin. Ithaca: Cornell University Press, 1980.

———. *Nouveau discours du récit.* Paris: Seuil, 1983.

———. *Palimpsestes.* Paris: Seuil, 1982.

———. "Vraisemblance et motivation." *Communications* 11 (1968): 5–21.

Gombrich, E. H. *Art and Illusion.* Bollingen Series. Princeton: Princeton Uni-versity Press, 1972.

Goodman, Nelson. "Twisted Tales; or, Story, Study, and Symphony." *Critical Inquiry* 7 (1980): 103–20.

———. *Ways of Worldmaking.* Indianapolis, Ind.: Hackett, 1978.

Graff, Gerald. "The Myth of the Postmodernist Breakthrough." *Tri-Quarterly* 26 (1973): 383–417.

Greismas, A. J., and J. Courtès. "The Cognitive Dimension of Narrative Discourse." *NLH* 7 (1976): 433–47.

Hamburger, Käthe. *Wahrheit und ästhetische Wahrheit*. Stuttgart: Klett and Cotta, 1979.

Hamon, Philippe. "Un Discours contraint." *Poétique* 16 (1974): 411–45.

Haverkamp, Anselm. "Allegorie, Ironie und Wiederholung." In *Text und Applikation*, Poetik und Hermeneutik 9, pp. 551–65. Munich: Fink Verlag, 1981.

———. "Illusion und Empathie: Die Struktur der 'teilnehmenden Lektüre' in den *Leiden Werthers*." In *Erzählforschung*, ed. Eberhard Lämmert, pp. 243–68. Stuttgart: Metzler, 1982.

Hirsch, Marianne. "A Mother's Discourse: Incorporation and Repetition in *La Princesse de Clèves*." *Yale French Studies* 62 (1981): 67–87.

Holland, Norman N. "Recovering 'The Purloined Letter': Reading as a Personal Transaction." In *The Reader in the Text: Essays on Audience and Interpretation*, ed. Susan R. Suleiman and Inge Crosman, pp. 350–70. Princeton: Princeton University Press, 1980.

Hutcheon, Linda. "Ironie et parodie: stratégie et structure." *Poétique* 36 (1978): 467–77.

———. *Narcissistic Narrative: The Metafictional Paradox*. Waterloo, Ontario: Wilfrid Laurier University Press, 1980.

Iser, Wolfgang. *The Act of Reading: A Theory of Aesthetic Response*. Baltimore: Johns Hopkins University Press, 1978.

———. *The Implied Reader: Patterns of Communication in Prose Fiction from Bunyan to Beckett*. Baltimore: Johns Hopkins University Press, 1974.

———. "Indeterminacy and the Reader's Response in Prose Fiction." In *Aspects of Narrative*, ed. J. Hillis Miller, pp. 1–45. New York: Columbia University Press, 1971.

Jauss, Hans Robert. *Ästhetische Erfahrung und literarische Hermeneutik*. Vol. 1. Munich: Fink Verlag, 1977.

———. *Aesthetic Experience and Literary Hermeneutics*. Trans. Michael Shaw. Minneapolis: University of Minnesota Press, 1982.

———. "Literary History as a Challenge to Literary Theory." In *New Directions in Literary History*, ed. Ralph Cohen, pp. 11–41. Baltimore: Johns Hopkins University Press, 1974.

Jefferson, Ann. *The Nouveau Roman and the Poetics of Fiction*. Cambridge: Cambridge University Press, 1980.

Johnson, Barbara. *The Critical Difference: Essays in the Contemporary Rhetoric of Reading*. Baltimore: Johns Hopkins University Press, 1980.

Kerbrat-Orecchioni, Catherine. "Le Texte littéraire: non-référence, auto-référence, ou référence fictionnelle?" *Texte*, no. 1 (1982): 27–49.

La Fayette, Madame de. *La Princesse de Clèves*. Ed. Alain Seznec. Cambridge, Mass.: Integral Editions, 1969.

———. *The Princess of Clèves*. Trans. anonymous. In *Seven French Short Novel Masterpieces*. New York: Popular Library, 1965.

Laugaa, Maurice. *Lectures de Mme de Lafayette*. Paris: Armand Colin, 1971.

Lewis, Thomas E. "Notes Toward a Theory of the Referent." *PMLA* 94, no. 3 (1979): 459–75.

Margolis, Joseph. "The Logic and Structures of Fictional Discourse." *Philosophy and Literature* 7 (1983): 162–81.

Miller, Nancy K. "Emphasis Added: Plots and Plausibilities in Women's Fiction." *PMLA* 96 (1981): 36–48.

Muller, Marcel. *Les Voix narratives dans "La Recherche du temps perdu."* Geneva: Librairie Droz, 1965.

Mulvey, Laura. "Visual Pleasure and Narrative Cinema." In *Women and the Cinema: A Critical Anthology*, ed. Karyn Kay and Gerald Peary, pp. 6–18. New York: Dutton, 1977.

Neef, Jacques. "La Figuration réaliste." *Poétique*, no. 16 (1973): 466–76.

Popper, Karl. "Naturgesetze und Theoretische Systeme." In *Theorie und Realität*. Ed. Hans Albert. Tübingen: Mohr, 1972.

Pratt, Mary Louise. *Toward a Speech Act Theory of Literary Discourse*. Bloomington: Indiana University Press, 1977.

Prince, Gerald. "Introduction à l'étude du narrataire." *Poétique* 14 (1973): 178–96.

Proust, Marcel. *A la recherche du temps perdu*. Bibliothèque de la Pléiade. 3 vols. Paris: Gallimard, 1954.

———. *Remembrance of Things Past*. 3 vols. Trans. C. K. Scott Moncrieff and Terence Kilmartin. New York: Random House, 1981.

Putnam, Hilary. "Is There a Fact of the Matter About Fiction?" Talk delivered at the MLA Convention, 29 December 1981, in New York.

Ricardou, Jean. "Proust: A Retrospective Reading." Trans. Erica Freiberg. *Critical Inquiry* 8 (1982): 531–41.

Ricoeur, Paul. *La Métaphore vive*. Paris: Seuil, 1975.

———. "Qu'est-ce qu'un texte?" In *Hermeneutik und Dialektik*. Festschrift in honor of H. G. Gadamer, ed. Rüdiger Bubner et al., 2: 181–200. Tübingen: Mohr, 1970.

———. *Temps et récit*. Vol. 1. Paris: Seuil, 1983.

———. *Temps et récit*. Vol. 2, *La configuration dans le récit de fiction*. Paris: Seuil, 1984.

———. *Temps et récit*. Vol. 3, *Le temps raconté*. Paris: Seuil, 1985.

Riffaterre, Michael. "Flaubert's Presuppositions." *Diacritics* 11 (1981): 2–16.

———. "Sade, or Text as Fantasy." *Diacritics* 2 (1972): 2–9.

———. *Semiotics of Poetry*. Bloomington: Indiana University Press, 1978.

———. "Sémiotique intertextuelle: l'interprétant." In *Rhétoriques, sémiotiques*, pp. 128–50. Collection 10/18. Paris: CNRS and Centre National des Lettres, 1979.

———. "La Syllepse intertextuelle." *Poétique*, no. 40 (1979): 496–501.

———. "La Trace de l'intertexte." *La Pensée*, no. 215 (1980): 4–18.

Rimmon-Kenan, Shlomith. "Paradoxical Status of Repetition." *Poetics Today* 1 (1980): 151–59.

Robbe-Grillet, Alain. "Order and Disorder in Film and Fiction." Trans. Bruce Morrissette. *Critical Inquiry* 4 (1977): 1–20.
———. *Pour un nouveau roman*. Collection Idées. Paris: Gallimard, 1963.
———. *Projet pour une révolution à New York*. Paris: Ed. de Minuit, 1970.
———. *Project for a Revolution in New York*. Trans. Richard Howard. New York: Grove Press, 1972.
———. "What Interests Me is Eroticism." Interview with Germaine Brée. In *Homosexualities and French Literature*, ed. George Stambolian and Elaine Marks, pp. 87–100. Ithaca: Cornell University Press, 1979.
Roloff, Volker. "Der Begriff der Lektüre in kommunikationstheoretischer und literaturwissenschaftlicher Sicht." *Romanistisches Jahrbuch* 29 (1979): 33–57.
———. "Empathie und Distanz: Überlegungen zu einem Grenzproblem der Erzähl-und Leserforschung (am Beispiel von Sartres *L'Idiot de la famille*). In *Erzählforschung*, ed. Eberhard Lämmert, pp. 269–89. Stuttgart: Metzler, 1982.
———. "Identifikation und Rollenspiel: Anmerkungen zur Phantasie des Lesers." *Zeitschrift für Literaturwissenschaft und Linguistik* 6 (1977): 260–76.
———. "Lecture et intertextualité: à propos de l'évolution du discours esthétique dans les *Cahiers* et dans *A la recherche du temps perdu*." *Bulletin d'Informations Proustiennes*, no. 13 (1982): 37–43.
———. *Werk und Lektüre: Zur Literaturästhetik von Marcel Proust*. Frankfurt: Insel Verlag, 1984.
Rousset, Jean. *Forme et signification*. Paris: Corti, 1964.
Searle, John R. "The Logical Status of Fictional Discourse." *New Literary History* 6 (1975): 319–32.
Smith, Barbara Herrnstein. "Contingencies of Value." *Critical Inquiry* 10 (1983): 1–35.
———. "Narrative Versions, Narrative Theories." *Critical Inquiry* 7 (1980): 213–36.
———. *On the Margins of Discourse: The Relation of Literature to Language*. Chicago: University of Chicago Press, 1978.
Sontag, Susan. *Against Interpretation*. New York: Farrar, Strauss and Giroux, 1966.
Suleiman, Susan Rubin. "The Question of Readability in Avant-Garde Fiction." *Studies in Twentieth-Century Literature* 6 (1981–1982): 17–35.
———. "Reading Robbe-Grillet: Sadism and Text in *Projet pour une révolution à New York*." *Romanic Review* 68 (1977): 43–62.
———. "Redundancy and the 'Readable' Text." *Poetics Today* 1 (1980): 119–42.
Todorov, Tzvetan. *Mikhaïl Bakhtine: le principe dialogique*. Paris: Seuil, 1981.
Updike, John. "Grove is My Press and Avant My Garde." *New Yorker*, 4 November 1967, pp. 223–38.
Uspensky, Boris. *A Poetics of Composition*. Trans. Valentina Zavarin and Susan Wittig. Berkeley: University of California Press, 1973.
Vaihinger, Hans. *Die Philosophie des Als Ob*. Leipzig: Felix Meiner, 1920.

Valincour, J. B. de. *Lettres à Madame la Marquise de*** sur le sujet de la Princesse de Clèves*. Ed. A. Cazes. Paris: Editions Bossard, 1926.

van Rossum–Guyon, Françoise. *Critique du roman*. Paris: Gallimard, 1970.

Vološinov, V. N. *Marxism and the Philosophy of Language*. Trans. Ladislav Matejka and I. R. Titunik. New York and London: Seminar Press, 1973.

Walton, Kendall L. "How Remote Are Fictional Worlds from the Real World?" *Journal of Aesthetics and Art Criticism* 37 (1978–1979): 11–23.

Weinrich, Harald. "Les Temps et les personnes." *Poétique* no. 39 (1979): 338–52.

Wellek, René. "Some Principles of Criticism." In *The Critical Moment*, pp. 41–42. London: Faber and Faber, 1963.

Wimmer, Rainer. *Referenzsemantik*. Tübingen: Max Niemeyer Verlag, 1979.

Woshinsky, Barbara. *La Princesse de Clèves: The Tension of Elegance*. The Hague: Mouton, 1973.

INDEX